W9-APX-540

COWLEY PUBLICATIONS is a ministry of the brothers of the
Society of Saint John the Evangelist, a monastic order in
the Episcopal Church. Our mission is to provide books and
resources for those seeking spiritual and theological formation. COWLEY PUBLICATIONS is committed to developing a new
generation of writers and teachers who will encourage people
to think and pray in new ways about spirituality, reconciliation, and the future.

Mark My Word

▼

Forty Days with Jesus
through the Eyes of St. Mark

RICHARD GILES

CꙨWLEY PUBLICATIꙨNS
Cambridge, Massachusetts

Published in the United States of America by Cowley Publications, a division of the Society of Saint John the Evangelist. No portion of this book may be reproduced, stored in or introduced into a retrieval system, or transmitted, in any form or by any means—including photocopying—without the prior written permission of Cowley Publications, except in the case of brief quotations embedded in critical articles and reviews.

Copyright © Richard Giles 1995
Originally published in English under the title
Mark My Word by the Canterbury Press Norwich of
9–17 St. Albans Place, London N1 0NX, UK

Library of Congress Cataloging-in-Publication Data

Giles, Richard, 1940–
   Mark my word : forty days with Jesus through the eyes of St. Mark /
Richard Giles.
      p. cm.
   Includes bibliographical references.
   ISBN 1-56101-239-4 (pbk. : alk. paper) 1. Bible. N.T.
Mark—Devotional use. 2. Jesus Christ—Biography—Meditations.
I. Title.
   BS2585.54.G55 2005
   242—dc22

                                                            2005019394

Scripture quotations are taken from the New Revised Standard Version of the Bible, © 1989, by the Division of Christian Education of the National Council of the Churches of Christ in the United States of America. Used by permission.

Cover design: Brad Norr Design
Cover art: Charles Perkalis
Interior design: Wendy Holdman

This book was printed in the United States of America on acid-free paper.

Cowley Publications
4 Brattle Street
Cambridge, Massachusetts 02138
800-225-1534 • www.cowley.org

*For Susan and Simone, who kept me going
through the writing of this book*

This little book arose from a series of addresses given at the
1994 Priests' Retreat at the Shrine of Our Lady of Walsingham,
Norfolk, England.

My warm thanks to Canon Martin Warner (the then Admin-
istrator), for inviting me to give the addresses in the first place,
and to Brother Raphael, SSF, for encouraging me (at some point
along the A17) to expand them into book form.

Richard Giles
Philadelphia
Feast of St. Mark 2005

Contents ▸

Mark My Word

▼

Day 1 ▶

MARK 1:1

The beginning of the good news of Jesus Christ,
the Son of God.

Who is this Jesus, who wanders onto center stage in this earliest of the Christian Gospels? This man who hears voices, who appears as someone possessed by the Spirit of God, who has only to look a person in the eye to cause him or her to abandon all to follow him?

The first verse is the only time in this Gospel where Mark himself refers to Jesus as "Son of God," and the old Revised Standard Version of the Scriptures casts doubt on the authenticity of the designation. So if we are to get under the skin of Mark's account, it may well be more in keeping with the spirit of his approach to lie low on the divine, to approach Jesus via the tradesman's entrance. Mark's account is a work of classic understatement. Matthew may have written for the Jews, but Mark wrote for the English (and for Episcopalians). So let's go along with the "other ancient authorities," omit "Son of God," and look simply at "the beginning of the good news of Jesus Christ."

No problem here with "the Christ"; Jesus is the one we have been waiting for, the Anointed One of God.

Precisely for this reason, Mark has no time for sensational birth stories with angelic fanfares; Jesus is introduced to us as a grown man, because he has a huge task ahead of him and time is short.

It was Austin Farrer who likened the Anglican Church to

a bra—"for uplift, for support, for ladies"—and nothing much has changed. This is probably how most non-Christians see most of the churches most of the time. We are genteel and ineffectual and meet in the afternoons. Certainly no place for macho types.

Mark sets the record straight. The story of Jesus is suitable for screening only on cable TV. It is a story of confrontation and violent upheaval; of revolution in relationships between mankind and God, and within the human race. The only kind of tea party appropriate to Mark's Gospel is a Boston Tea Party—the kind of prophetic act that ignites a revolution and gives birth to a new nation. China cups and cucumber sandwiches are definitely out. The reign of God is about to erupt into the world.

For us reading this story two millennia later, the explosion of God's love into the world is now recognized, not as a one-off event—a cataclysmic eruption of a volcano, which has remained dormant ever since—but as an explosion that has triggered a chain reaction of smaller explosions, unstoppable and unquantifiable.

The mystery of Jesus the fully human, the only human, emptied of self and filled with God, is not a secret buried deep in some Galilean archaeological site, but one that is revealed and shared every time an individual is stirred by the story of Jesus and, empowered by the Spirit of God, puts on his shoes and takes up his cross.

In so far as we enter into the life of Jesus the Christ, we too shall become sons and daughters of God. Wherever two or three gather and pray and celebrate and serve and are liberated in his name, our sad little world is irradiated with the fierce burning light of the love of God. The explosions never stop.

QUESTIONS:

Is my faith a grown-up faith? Or am I still hanging around in the children's corner clinging to my Sunday school pictures of God?

PRAYER:

O God, teach me, your child, to grow up into you in the strength of your Spirit. Help me not to make excuses or to blame others. Show me in Jesus how to come of age and take hold of my life, so that I may give it to you freely and joyfully, in the light and in the dark.

Day 2 ▶

MARK 1:2-8

John the baptizer appeared in the wilderness,
proclaiming a baptism of repentance for the forgiveness of sins.

Because he comes to do an impossible job, Jesus needs the proper introductions; to be planted firmly in the field of Jewish hopes and expectations.

First Isaiah introduces us to the introducer, John the baptizer, John the forerunner, John the announcer; the New Testament's very own wild man of God. Here is someone we would rather not have in our Bible study group; he is an embarrassment, an inconvenience. You never know what he is going to do next.

When I worked in Tyneside, in the northeast of England, we had our own "John the Baptizer"—who had given himself to the little-known ministry of rebuking. He would "rebuke in the name of the Lord" people in bus queues, tourists in the cafés down at the coast, or our local church community if he thought for a moment we were not subject to his version of the word of God. He loved God fiercely, but we were always glad when he went home. He kept us humble. John keeps us humble before God because his passion is God and nothing must stand in the way of God. These are the credentials of the "messenger . . . who will prepare your way." In living out the prophecy of Isaiah to "make his paths straight," John is a veritable steamroller of a man. There is no question of accommodation, compromise, or special deals; nothing must stand in the way of the work of God.

John Donne credits the apostles with the same unerring singleness of heart and mind; they are devoured by their message:

> So the apostles proceeded; when they came in their peregrination to a new State, to a new Court, to Rome itself, they did not enquire, how stands the Emperor affected to Christ, and to the preaching of his Gospel; is there not a sister, or a wife that might be wrought upon to further the preaching of Christ?
> This was not their way; they only considered who sent them; Christ Jesus: and what they brought; salvation to every soul that embraced Christ Jesus'.

"They only considered who sent them." That was their way; ours seems to be constantly preoccupied with the "rights of the listener"—to privacy, to consideration, to a hassle-free existence.

Recently I had cause to do a bit of shaking the dust from my feet on a parish doorstep; I believed that the hard word I had to say was an occasional necessary part of my work, but I felt so *guilty*! Surely the friendly neighborhood parish priest should remain mild-mannered at all times? Perhaps I should rush back and apologize? Will this mean a letter to the bishop from an outraged parishioner? In this way is the rough voice of prophecy within us planed down to smooth platitude.

If a terrorist device is about to explode in a nearby trash can, to alert passersby it is necessary to inconvenience them. They will thank us later. Warning the passersby cannot by definition be hassle-free. Here the message becomes everything; the sensibilities of the hearers or the safety of the messenger are of no account. John's listening skills remained undeveloped. He was not into counseling. John's message is too important for us to apologize away, too urgent for us to wrap up in polite conversation. There's no need for us to feel guilty about delivering it. Like the bomb ticking away in the trash can, self-centeredness and greed tick away in the human heart, and we have only the present moment in which to sound the alarm.

John's message begins with the hard word of "repentance for the forgiveness of sins," but once his hearers are hooked, he goes on to his real work of signposting:

> "The one who is more powerful than I is coming after me. . . . I have baptized you with water; but he will baptize you with the Holy Spirit."

The best is yet to come!

QUESTIONS:
How good am I at catching the attention of others for God? Having done so, how good am I at letting go, that they may be possessed by the Spirit of God?

PRAYER:

O God, help me, like John the forerunner, so to forget myself that your message may be alive in me and spoken through me, to prepare the way of Jesus in the power of your Spirit.

Day 3 ▶

MARK 1:9–13

"You are my Son, the Beloved; with you I am well pleased."

Without further ado, Jesus enters onto the stage. As with John, so with Jesus, the padding is kept to a minimum; let's just get on with the job.

The other evangelists give us sermon snippets of John, and hair-raising accounts of confrontations with the religious establishment. Where Jesus is concerned, the others give us genealogies, supernatural appearances, and dream sequences to spice up the story a little. It's an early example of media hype at full tilt.

Mark knows full well that all this is totally unnecessary. There is absolutely no need to know where Jesus came from or who his parents were. Very soon afterward, the early Church's PR department would be forced to give in to the pressure for further detail. Luke was on hand with his wonderful gift of storytelling to satisfy the demand of fans everywhere for minute detail of their hero's early life; while Matthew, clutching his concordance, did an admirable job proving to Jewish readers that Jesus' messianic credentials were impeccable from infancy onward. We are given a wealth of fantastic detail about Jesus' origins, not only human but divine.

But for Mark all that matters is that Jesus is here, and that he has work to do, and that he gets on with it.

> I am not interested in excuses for delay;
> I am interested only in a thing done.

These words were written by Jawaharlal Nehru, first prime minister of India, but they could well have come from Mark. Mark is the supreme pragmatist, and his account is of Jesus the workman, the craftsman who shapes the Kingdom of God with his bare hands.

Jesus is given totally to his work, because he is a man, The Man, totally possessed by the Spirit. His workmanship flows from his dream. For Jesus is a dreamer. He dreams of the Kingdom of God, of a different world order in which the hatreds of humanity are swallowed up in the love of God—a new alternative society, which Pope Paul VI called "the civilization of love." Jesus hears distinctly the voice of God speaking to him; he sees visions of heaven and of the Spirit of God descending on him.

In a way, which even he is reluctant to articulate, Jesus knows himself to be truly a son of God, his father's favorite: "You are my Son, the Beloved; with you I am well pleased." Jesus, from his first conscious moments, knows he is different, and grows steadily in awareness of the awful responsibility laid upon him. Jesus loves God his father with an aching of his soul, and senses from the moment of his anointing that his specialness enables him to enter into the agony of God beholding his lost creation.

This is immediately borne out by Jesus' desert experience.

Jesus feels himself driven out by the Spirit of God to grapple with forces of evil. This is the real battleground of life in which every individual ends up either slave or free: the battle for the mind. This is the world where the millionaire can live as an abject, hopeless prisoner, while the person with nothing can be rich beyond price. Jesus must win this battle to be free to lay down his life for God. Anointing from above must be accompanied by total surrender from below.

The West Point graduation leads directly and swiftly to Okinawa.

QUESTIONS:
Do I know myself to be a treasured child of God? If so, how do I use my privileged position?

PRAYER:
O God, anoint me with your Spirit, that I may dream dreams of your Kingdom here on earth, and in the pattern of Jesus, offer myself to you in complete surrender.

Day 4 ►

MARK 1:14–20

> *"The time is fulfilled, and the kingdom of God has come near; repent, and believe in the good news."*

Having been anointed, having sorted out the wild beasts of his imagination, Jesus gets down to work.

But not immediately. The kick-start for the inauguration

of Jesus' public ministry (hidden in half a verse we usually pass over) is the arrest of John the forerunner. Jesus must have bided his time, waiting for the signal. The removal of John from the scene meant he could wait no longer. The leading player had been carried off the field, and the new signing was ready at the goal line—his moment had come.

That simply is his message; the moment has come, not just for him but for all mankind: "The time is fulfilled, and the kingdom of God has come near." Do we participate in the game, or do we watch? Do we seize the opportunity to become a key player, or do we live out a lifetime on the substitutes' bench?

Now that the time has come, what does Jesus require of us? In the first instance he does not ask for dramatic action or intervention in events, but simply for two things, both welling up from within, where we can choose to be master or slave. The two things are *repentance* and *belief*. He demands that his hearers turn back to God, turning around their lives in the process, and that they believe the gospel, the good news.

Because somebody somewhere has subjected us to theological child abuse, being urged to "believe in the gospel" may well get us off to a bad start. We have come to understand "the gospel" as a set of dogmatic statements rather than as a way of life, so we will immediately start to worry about which bits of the Creed we find we cannot swallow. But if we move away from doctrines to attitudes, we see that to "believe the good news" is more a question of a basic disposition of the heart: to believe the best about people, to look on the bright side, to live hopefully and with awe and wonder, to be constantly thankful to our gracious God, and, secure in our Father's love, to pursue the truth fearlessly, knowing that "[nothing] will be able to separate us from the love of God" (Romans 8:39).

Through the preaching of Jesus, we see that the good news is about understanding God, for the first time, as accessible, loving, merciful, generous, patient, and kind. In other words we see in Jesus the good news that God is not, after all, the stern teacher or the cold, dutiful stepfather; he's "Dad." What's more, he has no favorites. We can all, without exception, become his cherished sons and daughters, loved to bits.

The effect of this good news breaking in on the lives of those who first heard the preaching of Jesus was like the first rain after years of drought. His words made rich, fertile soil out of a desert. A gang of fishermen—for whom life offered nothing but sweat and tears and (on a good week) a drink in the bar on a Friday night—suddenly saw the point of it all. Life overflowed with the reality of God. They were under new management.

These first followers of Jesus had found their vocation—that which they were always meant to be. Not vocation as a pious resolution in a flower-filled retreat house, but what Bishop John Robinson described as "the same constricting and exhausting effect that makes you want to clutch your head and bite your lips."

We can tell that it wasn't merely a question of words. Jesus mesmerized them, captivated them, intoxicated them, made them laugh, made them hang awestruck upon his every word, made them feel like a million dollars. Absolutely nothing would be allowed to stop them from going with this man who was the first real man they had ever met, a man full of God.

QUESTIONS:

Have I found my vocation? Do I know myself to be taken over by God? If so, for what purpose, in what role, am I to serve God?

PRAYER:

O God, let the gospel of Jesus be to me good news, that I may live without fear of others or of myself and generously share that love so lavished upon me in your Spirit.

Day 5 ▶

MARK 1:21–28

They were astounded at his teaching, for he taught them
as one having authority, and not as the scribes.

Immediately is a very Markan word. Almost everything for Mark happens immediately after the previous event. There is no hanging around, no waiting for the rain to clear or for the umpires to inspect the pitch. Play must continue, and without a break. Mark is a man who celebrates the meaning of *now*. He would have gotten on well with the late Dennis Potter, who, with only a few weeks to live, rejoiced that "the **nowness** of everything is absolutely wondrous."

Mark found it "absolutely wondrous" that Jesus takes control, and that he takes it now, in this moment. "The present moment," wrote Jean-Pierre de Caussade, "is the ambassador who declares the order of God," and Jesus now fills to bursting each moment with the vigor of his irrepressible and boundless life. Mark knows with every fiber of his body the truth that

> Bliss was it in that dawn to be alive
> but to be young was very heaven.

William Wordsworth wrote those words in "The Prelude" about the French Revolution, but the revolution that Jesus sets alight is no temporary political upheaval but an eternal change in the relationship between humankind and God. Nothing will ever be the same again.

This is Jesus' first "public appearance," and he leaves nothing to chance. No one is to be left in any uncertainty about his intentions. For location he chooses a town in his home territory; for venue, the synagogue; for timing, a Sabbath day. Everything is sharpened to a single point, at which Jesus will take on the religious establishment of his day.

Ched Myers, in his commentary on Mark, *Binding the Strong Man,* brings the Greek of verse 21 alive for us when he says Jesus "strides" into the synagogue. Although Jesus is taking his place at the heart of his own religious culture, he comes no longer as a mere member but as a leader, like a bishop taking possession of his cathedra (the bishop's chair) in the same building where he once sang as a boy chorister. Make no mistake, this is no ambling Sunday routine, a taking of a seat near the back in case one needs to slip out before the end; this is a grand entrance. It is an entrance appropriate to an anointed Son of God, a messiah.

Jesus has come to teach. Evidently he has already established himself as a religious teacher of some sort and, like the seminarian asked to preach in his own parish when he's home from college, the regulars at Capernaum wait expectantly to see what this local boy is made of.

The immediate reaction is one of astonishment. Why? Because Jesus speaks with authority, a natural authority flowing from total integrity, the mark of a man utterly at peace with himself and with his God. Thomas Merton called our attention to this most vital of all conquests: "What can we gain by sailing to the moon" he wrote, "if we are not able to cross the abyss that separates us from ourselves?"

In Jesus there is no abyss; external appearance and inward reality are identical. There is no yawning gap between what he is and what he wishes to be. He has made the will of God his own. This is why he alone can speak with authority. Mark tells us that this is astonishing precisely because it is in marked contrast to the regular diet of teaching dished out by the scribes. They are professionals, and this is their job rather than their life. Like all professionals, they become so adept at using words effectively and cleverly that the meaning no longer takes hold of them; they become a freight train of empty box cars, rattling by.

Jesus' authority is invincible because it comes from within. It requires no authentication from outside, no external status or important-sounding title, no ticket, no countersignature. Jesus is who he is. God is "I AM WHO I AM" (Exodus 3:14).

QUESTIONS:

How can we begin to grow into total integrity, as individuals and as communities? What is the first small step in crossing the abyss that separates me from myself?

PRAYER:

O God, by your Spirit may your will be mine, so that I may show to others no longer a facade but the reality and authority of your love alive in me, in the pattern of Jesus your Son.

Day 6 ▶

MARK 1:29—2:17

In the morning, while it was still very dark, he got up and went out to a deserted place, and there he prayed. . . . When he returned to Capernaum . . . so many gathered around that there was no longer room for them, not even in front of the door.

Popular magazines specialize in "stories behind the headlines" because we are all insatiably curious about what makes people tick: how celebrities relax at home, what kind of house they live in, what breed of dog sits at their feet.

Mark doesn't let us down. Once the "launch ceremony" is over, we are rushed over (again "immediately") to Capernaum, to peek behind the doors of the lakeside home of Mr. and Mrs. Bar Jonah, where Jesus, having taken the town by storm, can now be found relaxing with friends. This change of scene has about it a delightful domesticity, which only serves to sharpen the authenticity of the gospel's story. No inventor of a world religion would take his hero from center stage direct to a kitchen scene complete with a mother-in-law! It is too prosaic for words; too real, too natural, to have been made up. Here is Jesus sitting at a crowded kitchen table, dirty washing hurriedly moved to make room for him, a milk carton at his elbow ("I can never open these things!" says Simon, all fingers and thumbs), children's toys at his feet, a dog sniffing his sandals.

The inauguration of Jesus' ministry at Capernaum is followed by a period of intense activity in which the authority of his teaching is authenticated in action—healings, and releasing people from the powers that possessed them, whether sin, darkness, or despair. His words bear fruit in action, whereas we too often are content with mere words. We have the hymnbooks but we don't sing the music; "words only" it says on our cover.

Jesus' activity is not one long, unbroken ministry marathon, but is interspersed with two other equally important activities: relaxation and solitary prayer, two strands woven into the fabric of his life's work.

Relaxing with friends (1:29) was as important to Jesus as praying to the Father. Here he was putting in the footings of the new building that would become that invincible world community, which St. Paul was later to christen "the Body of Christ." Here he was, accepting love, cherished by those who would die for him. Borne up by the excited adulation of his first followers ("Boss, you were awesome today!"), Jesus is able to harness their childlike enthusiasms, correct their misunderstandings, and foster their first inklings of the truth.

But Jesus could not keep going for long before escaping to be quite alone (1:35), to immerse himself in the presence of God. Usually this was in the early morning, when darkness and silence combine to seduce our senses with the wonder of our littleness in the hand of God, and the miracle of each new magical dawn. (G. K. Chesterton found one new day such an incredible gift that he thought it amazing that we are allowed two.) Here at dawn we are brought face-to-face with the delight of God in his creation, with Evelyn Underhill's insight that God's creativity is "not by mechanical necessity, but by passionate desire." If we're never up early to pray (and that may mean simply being still, gazing in wonder at it all), then we are utterly stupid.

We note, however, that Jesus is not on retreat. There are no separate compartments; there is no little notice on the door that says "Engaged" to protect the private encounter. Jesus is interrupted constantly and mercilessly. When evening comes, just at the point when you feel it's time to get out the Scrabble board, Jesus finds that "the whole city was gathered together around the door," clamoring for healing and help. Next morning, no sooner is Jesus settled down to some quiet, serious prayer in a lonely spot, than Simon comes crashing through the undergrowth, cursing the thorns, and hollering to his companions, breathlessly announcing to a deep-sighing master that "everyone is searching for you."

It may be depressing for us to think that Jesus is never off duty (Is that the act we have to follow?), but for him it is not like that; the traffic is two-way. Jesus at prayer, Jesus relaxing at home, never ceases to reveal the love and power of God. Jesus, teaching, healing, confronting, never ceases to be the man of prayer, the man with time for his friends, seeing the funny side, enjoying each mouthful of food, savoring the wine, as he sits in the tavern with the tax collectors and sinners. He is neither "on duty" nor "off duty"; he is simply himself. His life is a unity.

QUESTIONS:
What are the dominant threads that give color and texture to the fabric of my life? Is there a good mixture, giving interest and strength?

PRAYER:
O God, help me to see in Jesus the meaning of unity, that when I am dragged away from what seems important, I may constantly abide in your perfect will, embraced by your ever present Spirit.

Day 7 ▶

MARK 2:18–22

> *Jesus said to them, "The wedding guests cannot fast while the bridegroom is with them, can they?"*

"Some people are never satisfied" springs to mind when we think of the popular response to Jesus and to John who announced him, and the same applies to our own generation. If you don't want to do something you know is right, play for time, ask a question, be awkward.

The knack employed is never to accept and enjoy people for what they are, but to point out the differences with their predecessor or opposite number, getting an argument going where there is none. The last parish priest was "a hopeless old bungler"; his replacement "nothing more than a business-man." John was a religious crank, Jesus a playboy.

To the questioners in this case, overconcerned with the niceties of religious practice, Jesus gives a reply that stresses the celebratory role of his presence with us. Fasting is inappropriate for his followers because he is to them a bride-groom before the wedding; the people of God are partying, and Jesus is not going to spoil the fun. All too soon will come the time for fasting and mourning and tears. We are far too interested in checking things out—the priest's seminary, the soundness of her sermons, the color of his socks—ever to let go and enjoy ourselves. So busy asking the right questions, we forget that God is trying to throw a party and give us a good time. Rose Macaulay reminds us that "God himself cannot give us back a lost party." Just how many parties have we missed, as with our arrogant questions we spat upon God's bounty? Samuel Johnson was once told by a friend, "I have tried to be a philosopher, but cheerfulness keeps breaking through." We may often try to be religious, but always the joy of Jesus bursts in, mocking our prim, pious questions of decency and order.

There are many experts to tell us about Jesus and his intentions as regards the Jewish faith: was he a Jewish reformer or the innovator of a new deal with God? Perhaps the great apostasy of the Christian movement was not after all the cozy arrangement with Constantine, but the first congregation to abandon any attempt to hold in unity the old and new dispensations of God's grace. Who knows?

All that Jesus tells us here is that we are always going to have trouble keeping bubbly new wine in old containers. Religious movements, like humankind in general, can bear only so much reality. The Jewish establishment couldn't contain Jesus any more than the Roman Catholic system could contain Martin Luther; the Anglican, John Wesley; or the Methodist, William Booth. It's bad enough being born again; don't ask us to do it a *second* time.

What matters is not our faithfulness to an inherited creed, a cultural mold, a received wisdom, but our fearless exploration of God, of truth, of reality, in the explosion of the present moment. Christian maturity lies in being open to God now, no matter what offense or disappointment that may give rise to in others. We have nothing to fear from the truth. We need fear only the consequences of making do with anything less than the truth, however considerate or compassionate our motive. As John Robinson put it, "the Christian is free to follow the truth *wherever* it leads."

QUESTIONS:

How ready am I to try new things, explore new paths, in my pilgrimage to God? Is my faithfulness to my tradition a genuine expression of a desire for God, or an evasion of God's demands upon me?

PRAYER:

O God, pour into me the new wine of your Spirit, that, like Jesus bursting from the tomb, I may walk free from all that holds me back in serving you.

Day 8 ▶

MARK 2:23—3:6

Then he said to them, "Is it lawful to do good or to do harm on the sabbath, to save life or to kill?"

Celebration, healing, deliverance, and reconciliation don't get you very far in a world that is only happy being miserable. Those who stay away from the party hear the noise, talk themselves into believing they had never been invited in the first place, and call the police.

The stay-at-homes in Mark's story are those professional religious people who resented Jesus' burgeoning spiritual influence, which they had no hope of containing. His fame and popularity increased daily, and they began to feel disregarded and marginalized. They had the titles and the framed certificates on their consulting room wall, but Jesus had the power. Something had to be done.

So it was that the nit-picking began. Every move Jesus made seemed to be monitored on a screen at the Pharisees' Mission Control. The minute Jesus said or did anything, scribes armed with clipboards seemed to leap out from behind the nearest rock, to challenge, to complain, to carp. First it was the innocent, unthinking act of his disciples, catching hold of stray ears of grain, nibbling at the husks, as they took a country stroll on the Sabbath day. This was reconstructed by the religious authorities as committing an offense. A natural, instinctive, harmless act was made into a sin against God.

Jesus bears with this patiently, beating them at their own

game by revealing his deeper knowledge of the Scriptures, and giving them a little *bon mot,* which they could go away with and ponder (and whip themselves up into a frenzy about). Looking at our own spiritually bankrupt generation, with its tragic belief in 24/7 shopping as the pinnacle of human achievement and happiness, Jesus would have been the first to recall us to the good sense in this loving provision of God. The Sabbath insight is another means of helping us to love, by forcing us to make space and time for God. It reminds us that we are not machines for getting and spending, but incredibly beautiful and intricate human beings with a capacity for wonder and worship, which needs to be used and developed.

But the Sabbath is a means, not an end. In the final account, such structures are there to help us in our journey toward God, not to load onto us yet another oppressive burden. Human beings remain responsible and accountable for how they make use of the Sabbath; the tail cannot wag the dog. Therefore Jesus, as the representative human, can claim for himself, and for all who are willing to be remade in him, lordship of the Sabbath, as of any other mechanism designed by God to help humankind.

However godly our structures and props and routines, however biblical, however hallowed by unbroken tradition, they remain merely tools of the trade, Sabbaths over which we are master.

I remember how, as a hotheaded young curate outdoing my rector in blind obedience to Holy Church, I once eagerly entered into my notebook of quotations the words of Tertullian praising "the faith which has believed in the duty of complying with the rule, before it has learned the reason of it."

It's taken me some time to understand the fact that those who live by the rule book will perish by the rule book, and that, if we follow that road to its ultimate conclusion, we end up in a breakaway sect or an ecclesiastical time warp.

The second incident in the growing conflict of Jesus with the religious authorities is more serious. Here we touch, not on a concept but on a creature, a child of God with "a withered hand."

There is no dialogue here between Jesus and those who opposed him. They were watching his every move; Jesus could foresee their reaction, could write the script for them. It is a confrontation all the more violent because no words are spoken. Only looks were exchanged, and "if looks could kill," then several fatalities would have resulted from this incident.

At this point we wave good-bye to the Jesus we met in Sunday school. Here is Jesus driven to "anger" and "grief" at what religious people would do in the name of God. When all the powers of God to restore and make whole are available to a broken man at the hands of Jesus, when the people of God are gathered together on the Lord's day in the Lord's house, the wrench is thrown into the works by the very people who are supposedly on God's side. Those who know the laws of God inside out are the first to sabotage his plan to flood creation with his love. All this from vested interest on the part of those who have lost, somewhere in the small print of their rule book, the God who invented reading and made the reader.

In this angry confrontation, Jesus goes too far. For love of a man with a withered hand, he burns his boat and awaits his fate at the hands of those who from now on will scheme for his destruction.

QUESTIONS:

At what point in my pilgrimage do I lose sight of God in the small print of my rule book? How would Jesus look at me, no words being spoken?

PRAYER:
O God, keep alive in me your Holy Spirit, that I may never be a stumbling block to others on their journey to you in Jesus our Lord.

Day 9 ▸

MARK 3:7–19a

> *Whenever the unclean spirits saw him, they fell down before him and shouted, "You are the Son of God!"*

After confrontation, withdrawal. After the emotional violence of the synagogue, Jesus retreats to the coast, and lines up a contingency plan to escape from the crowds by sea, as and when necessary. Because he is a realist, and a strategist, he gets his disciples to organize a "getaway boat." Jesus lays down his life for his friends, but at the right time and place, not in an unnecessary accident on a beach but when the forces of good and evil come to fight their final battle at Golgotha. Until then he must keep himself in reserve, cunning as well as innocent in his struggle to open up humankind to the love of God.

Jesus is almost trampled to death on the shore as the crowds "pressed upon him to touch him." Significantly it is not in the adulation of his adoring fans that Jesus is recognized, but in the heartrending cries of those released by him from possession by unclean spirits.

No doubt today we would understand these lost souls as suffering from problems of mental health. If so, we know how often mentally disturbed people can share with children that freedom from inhibition, from pretence or sophistication, which enables them to speak the truth without fear or favor. While the "normal" mature adult considers all the options, flicking through a theological dictionary for the correct phraseology, the child or the mentally disabled person will have got it hours ago: "You are the Son of God!"

A Tyneside priest with a great pastoral heart once told me that a parish won't begin to get anywhere until it has in its congregation "a woman in a wheelchair and a mad boy." How desperately we all need "a mad boy," shouting out in the services and throwing the odd hymnbook, to keep us close to God. They know what's what when the spiritual chips are down. They know a person who is full of God when they see one.

Jesus withdraws further—this time into the hills again—when he gets down to the business of appointing his inner circle of helpers. He calls to him "those whom he wanted." Not the best or most suitable or most eager; not those who always have their hands up throughout the lesson or who carry his bags; not those who fit into correct political categories or will attract local government grants—but simply those whom he happened to want.

We all know how painful it can be to be left off the invitation list, but that only sharpens the joy at those moments in life when we are picked out, invited, specially chosen.

Jesus knew about sheep and goats, about separation and choice. He knew how vital it was for us to be *wanted for ourselves,* to be chosen. Up on that hillside there will have been disappointed candidates, but other opportunities would arise for them to serve God in due course, for "not one of them was lost" (John 17:12). For the moment, however, Jesus needs twelve special individuals, and he's going to have the ones he wants. Such is their task that they are going to need to feel special. The desire of God for them is the one thing that will keep them going even unto death.

For us now, disciples in our own generation, it is by our baptism that we are enlisted among the chosen of God. Martin Luther said that "in time of doubt I do not say 'I have believed' but 'I have been baptized.'" He knew that it is never what we do but what God does that counts. God is the lover, we the beloved. We are wanted for ourselves. We are chosen not because we are best qualified or most suitable, but simply because God desires us.

And that goes even for Judas.

QUESTIONS:
When do I make time to withdraw to be alone with God? How jealously do I guard my time with God?

PRAYER:
O God, at the times I feel furthest from you, remind me of your desire for me in the call of Jesus and the anointing of your Spirit in baptism.

Day 10 ▶

MARK 3:19b–30

> *When his family heard it, they went out to restrain him, for people were saying, "He has gone out of his mind."*

"Then he went home." This is only half a verse, but it says it all. Jesus is inaugurating a revolution in humanity's relationship to God, battling with the powers of evil, recruiting twelve men to change the world . . . and then he goes home. Nothing could be more ordinary, more familiar to us. We know the power of home to "restore, support, strengthen, and establish" us (1 Peter 5:10). Whether we've just seen our only child graduate with honors, or witnessed our beloved team's humiliating home defeat in the play-offs, our instinct is the same; whenever we feel emotionally exhilarated or drained, elated or shattered, there comes a moment when we say, "Let's go home."

Jesus is no exception. He needed to put his feet up, to lounge in his favorite chair, to be reassured by four familiar walls, the family photographs, and the crack in the plaster over the fireplace. Above all he needed someone to brew him a good cup of coffee.

"The home is the abiding place; in the home there is reality" wrote Kabir, and that deep truth applied to Jesus no less than to the rest of us. Whatever the Pharisees were plotting out there, whatever troubled spirits wailed in the night, here was home. Here for the moment he was safe and secure. Small wonder then that he chooses the picture of breaking and entering a house to describe, in answer to the scribes' challenge, the process of penetrating to the heart of Satan's kingdom.

The fact that the crowds gave him no peace, practically no time to enjoy being at home, only serves to heighten his appreciation of the ordinary, everyday pleasures of life. Mark tells us, such was the insistent pressure of the crowds that Jesus' household "could not even eat." Jesus is no John the baptizer; locusts and wild honey were not his scene at all. For him a nice piece of steak with lashings of sauce and a cup or two of local red wine would be just the ticket. Jesus is no automaton kept alive with regular injections of protein. He enjoys his food, and often, in the middle of a heavy session with his disciples, not all of whom are terribly bright, his thoughts must have wandered to what was for supper that night.

And Jesus had *friends*! Perhaps the most astonishing verse

in this passage is verse 21, which (in the King James transla-
tion) speaks of his friends who "went out to restrain him, for
people were saying, 'He has gone out of his mind.'" Yes, we know
about his family, his disciples, his other followers, but it somehow comes as a revelation to us that Jesus actually had friends.
People who were not tied to him by blood, not appointed by
him as "official" helpers, not self-appointed as camp followers,
but friends. People who loved him and cared about him, who
had known him long before he became famous, who thought
nothing more of him because of his celebrity status, and who
found this campaign of his a pain because of what it was doing
to him and to their schedule of regular nights out together.

This gives us a new dimension for our picture of Jesus, no
longer totally alone (back to the Sunday school version!) but
part of a normal human network of love and support. These
were true friends moreover, not afraid to take him to task when
appropriate or, as in this instance, to bodily remove him from
the crowds threatening to crush him. Even a revolutionary
prophet needs friends who know what's best for him and who
will completely take over when the necessity arises. These are
the kind of friends Jesus had.

Jesus' words on the unforgivable sin against the Holy Spirit
are frightening, but they healthily redirect our attention from
our catalogue of offenses, however dreadful or "unforgivable"
in the world's eyes, to basic attitudes. What Jesus denounces
here is the terrifying mind-set into which truth can never pene-
trate. We see it most often when people's minds and hearts become possessed by a single political ideology, whether within
a church or on a national stage, when closed minds travel with
increasing speed down the rail lines of bigotry and hatred. This
was the sin that destroyed Jesus; the sin that returned love with
hatred, that abandoned integrity, despised truth, and denied

our very nature as human beings. The sin against the Holy Spirit was the sin against the Son of God, and the sin against the Father himself.

QUESTIONS:
In what attitudes and preconceptions do I come dangerously close to committing the sin against the Holy Spirit? What sort of friend to Jesus am I?

PRAYER:
O God, save me from the sin against your Spirit by reminding me always that to believe in you is to believe in the world, in life, in humanity, in justice, in beauty, and in goodness, through Jesus your Son.

Day 11 ▶

MARK 3:31–35

> *And looking at those who sat around him, he said,*
> *"Here are my mother and my brothers!"*

Families! Is our family circle a joy to us or an embarrassment? Do we dread Christmas reunions or count off the days in eager anticipation? For Jesus it was a bit of both.

Jesus' mother was of course one of the best. Dad had died some years back, and she had had quite a struggle ever since. Never once did she abandon this strange son, even though he remained a mystery to her. She could never understand him, but knew from the beginning that he was different. All that homework, when he should have been out kicking a ball around with the other boys on the block; all those times he disappeared for hours on end, apparently for long solitary walks; that "distance" he maintained, even with her, despite his obvious filial devotion. For all this she loved him to the end, right up to Golgotha, where the worst thing of all was the laughter.

Her heart was big enough, not only for Jesus, but for all those he brought home with him. She became mother to them all. She bathed their grazed knees, provided a shoulder to cry on when they got to the girlfriend stage, and washed their football jerseys. For their part, they not only loved her, they respected her and listened to her. Later there was always to be a seat of honor kept for her in the inner councils of the infant Church.

His brothers were altogether different. Jealousy was their main problem, and you could see why. They had to sweat all day keeping the family joinery business going, while Jesus was neither use nor ornament. When he didn't have his head stuck in a book, he was out on the hillside behind the house, practicing sermons to imaginary crowds, hearing voices and talking to God.

Somehow Mom always seemed to take his side. Jesus always got the best cuts of meat on Sundays, and sometimes was allowed to skip washing up. Yes, he was different all right, but it was all so unfair. When the story of Joseph son of Jacob—he of the Gap catalog—came around in the readings at the synagogue, they could well sympathize with Simeon, Levi, Judah, and the rest of Joseph's brothers. When Jesus began to be famous, and the crowds came nosing around and barging in, it was all too much to take. If Jesus' brothers could have persuaded him to go to Egypt—to sort out *that* lot and to leave them in peace—they would have willingly gone in together for a one-way ticket.

When it came to the public holiday, when simply everyone went up to Jerusalem, the author of John's Gospel tells us that he plainly refused to go, dragging up some excuse that "my time has not yet come" (John 7:6). A fine messiah he was turning out to be!

On this occasion related by Mark, the family has had enough. Mother is worried sick, and the brothers are fed up with him causing all this commotion and distress. They come to interrupt this highfalutin talk of Satan and the Holy Spirit, this spiritual circus, to talk some sense into him and get him to come home.

Of course they cannot get near him, but a message is relayed to Jesus, telling him that his mother and brothers are waiting outside. We now witness the first-ever use of the classic "in conference" evasion strategy. Jesus is "in conference" healing and teaching and changing the world, and he cannot be interrupted, not even for his beloved mother and exasperating brothers.

This is astonishing reading for those who last met Jesus in their kindergarten years. It is so *unchristian* to talk like that! Surely it can't be Jesus talking about his mother that way? Surely Christianity is all about families round the fireside, charades at Christmas, and Saturday outings?

No, Jesus reveals here our true relationship to family under God. He loves his family, but they come second. That really says it all. Ever since that incident in Jerusalem (Luke 2:41–52) when, aged only 12, he disappeared and caused his parents so much anguish; he had been saying that he had another father, another family, to whom he owed prior allegiance.

Important as our families are, we are bound with far closer ties to those who stand alongside us around God's altar, whose lives are woven with ours into the tapestry of the will of God. We may not have known them long, we may have nothing at all in common with them except our shared calling, but they are our brothers and sisters whom we will love through death and beyond, those for whom Jesus commands us to lay down our lives. "*Here* are my mother and my brothers!"

QUESTIONS:
Who comes first in my hierarchy of loyalties? Who do I think of as my real family? What are the differences between my relationship with my natural family and my Church family?

PRAYER:
O God, Jesus shows us how to honor our father and mother, to lay down our lives for our friends, and to love you above all things. Help us, by your Spirit, to do the same.

Day 12 ▶

MARK 4:1–33

> *Such a very large crowd gathered around him that he got into a boat on the sea and sat there, while the whole crowd was beside the sea on the land.*

It was one of those days when the Sea of Galilee was like a millpond. It was early morning, and everything was sharp and radiant and clear, before the sun rose higher in the sky to flatten everything under its searing heat. The air was still, and the voice of Jesus carried clearly over the limpid water, echoing round the bay, bouncing off the low cliffs.

Despite the early hour, a large crowd had already gathered, and Jesus had commandeered a boat as a kind of floating podium from which he could address the crowd without being mobbed by them. Many of the youngsters had entered the water, hanging onto the mooring ropes, pushing each other under the surface and generally playing the fool, but stopping to listen more and more as the words of Jesus bore into them, their elders no longer needing to restrain them. Most of the crowd remained on the beach and around the cliff edge of the bay, very still and straining every muscle to lose not a single syllable drifting across the water.

Jesus had but a short time to live and much to tell. How could he get his message across quickly and effectively? His first teaching technique is to use picture language. He knew full well that we all have pictorial minds, that we like newsprint to be interspersed with photographs, and books with plenty of pictures. He knew that we may not be able readily to assimilate an abstract theological concept, but that all of us can easily grasp hold of a picture drawn from everyday life, and later apply its message as the truth of it sinks in.

If we can but start with a character, even a caricature, that makes us think or makes us laugh, we can then at our leisure, insofar as we are open to God, slowly recognize whom that character represents—perhaps it's me! (Yes, I know about v. 12, which makes not a scrap of sense, given Jesus' obvious intention to teach and explain. The experts tell us this is Mark rather than Jesus, feeling puzzled and depressed about the lack of success of Jesus' mission among his own people, which only became apparent later, and also getting a little mixed up about different meanings of the word here translated as "parable," which can mean either an illustrative story or a riddle. So let's leave that verse with Isaiah, where it originally came from).

Most of the crowd listening that morning knew about sowing seed. Outside their back doors they had little patches of bare earth, which passed for gardens, where a goat was tethered and a few chickens scratched about. Each year they would with renewed enthusiasm, hope triumphing over experience, sow a few packets of vegetable seeds, carefully saving the washing-up water to get them going. They knew all about stony ground and thistles.

So instead of delivering a dissertation on the effectiveness of the spoken word in theological teaching, he tells them a story. It is a story about someone doing what they do every year—sowing seed—and discovering what they rediscover every year: that it's a miracle that anything ever grows at all.

They enjoy the story because it's their world, their reality. They can identify with it immediately; they can walk into the picture, feeling the frustration and disappointment of the sower, delighting in his eventual good crop from the pocket of good soil. (Perhaps this year will be better for them too!)

The meaning would sink in as and when they opened their hearts to the word of God. For those willing to hear, they might one night go to bed pondering this story about a man sowing seed, and wake up to glimpse for the first time the wonder of God's patient sowing of his love in our lives. Jesus pops the penny into place; all we have to do is let it drop.

The poor disciples of course, being remedial pupils, a bit slow on the uptake, have to have some private coaching from Jesus later. They are usually the last to catch on. Quite justifiably he tells them (v. 13) that if they can't grasp this simple picture story, then they are going to be in real trouble when they get to their finals. Other vivid pictures followed that morning as the sun rose higher in the sky, and the crowd grew as more and more people heard what was going on and came running round the headland, and the sweat glistened more profusely on the faces of the audience. Handkerchiefs were dipped into the sea to cool those likely to faint, and boys were sent back to the village for jars of drinking water.

Jesus went on to talk about the lamp, which was brought

into the house in the evening to fill it with light; about the miracle of the ear of wheat, coming from a single grain; about the tiny mustard seed, giving birth to a tree big enough for birds to nest in its shade. These were fascinating insights into the world around them; pictures that gradually revealed insights into the workings of God and his dealings with us. Vincent van Gogh said of William Shakespeare that his language was "an artist's brush, quivering with fever and emotion." Jesus too is the supreme artist of language, the celebrant of a sacrament of words and pictures conveying to us the reality of eternal life.

QUESTIONS:
In this passage, which picture is most powerful in helping me to glimpse the purpose of God? Can I draw a picture from my own everyday experience in which I can also discern the purpose of God?

PRAYER:
O God, help me by your Spirit to see behind the detail to the point where you touch my life and change it, through Jesus, our teacher and painter.

Day 13 ►

MARK 4:35–41

He said to them, "Let us go across to the other side."

At the end of yet another tumultuous, exhausting day, Jesus uses the sea as a means of escape, putting some distance between himself and those who would drain him dry. "Let us go across to the other side."

"Crossing over" also has a deeper significance for Jesus and his disciples in the context of their own society. The western side of the Sea of Galilee was thoroughly Jewish, the eastern side around the Decapolis, the Ten Towns, a Hellenistic region. Mark doesn't seem to have majored in geography—his accounts of the crisscrossing of the lake by Jesus and his disciples do not correspond too well with the map—but nevertheless he's trying to tell us something important here.

Jesus is crossing over from one culture to another. France is only a few miles from England, but crossing over (or under) those few miles involves a culture leap as great as traveling to the other side of the planet. Language, landscape, architecture, food and drink, ambience: it is all delightfully different. No less for Jesus; in crossing over to the other side, he was entering a different culture, a culture that was to become the incubator of the infant Church—but that will come later.

Our first question to people on arrival is usually "Did you have a good journey?" Journeys, crossings, and transfers are important to us. They are a necessary interval between events in our lives; they place an important distance between experiences, a gap, a breathing space. Even in this country where regional differences are fast being eroded, we can enjoy sitting back on a plane out of Philadelphia, putting behind us those Philly cheese steaks as we speed toward different delicacies awaiting us on the Gulf, in the Midwest, or on the Pacific coast.

The architect responsible for the restoration of the ancient Orthodox monastery of Konevets, set on an island in Lake Lagoda, north of St. Petersburg, Russia, describes how vital the crossing over is for pilgrims coming to find God there: "Simply launching out into Lake Lagoda, you begin a process of cleansing. Once on the island, you look at your soul in a different way, and begin to look differently on the problems you left behind." The Cuban refugees fleeing across the Florida Straits know the truth of that too—as a matter of life and death.

Jesus, for the moment, had had enough of Capernaum and needed change. He wanted to bask in the contrast of another culture, another scene, to hear a different language, to eat some different food. *Vive la différence!* He wanted to send postcards from places his folks back home had never even heard of, and to buy some local bits and pieces his mother would really love. He wanted to get away, and he wanted to go now, not even bothering to go back to throw a few things in a suitcase: "They took him with them in the boat, just as he was."

In doing so, Jesus undertakes a symbolic journey of reconciliation between two cultures alien to each other. From now on, different societies approaching life and God in very different ways will share a common experience of the teaching and ministry of Jesus. They will each make of it what they will, and significantly, those with less of an ecclesiastical axe to grind will make much more of it than those immunized by generations of religious formation. Jesus lays down his life wherever he can within the confines of his geographical world, and each person who hears, who listens, who ponders these things in her heart, and who says yes to God, will, irrespective of background or culture, take it up again.

The crossing is not always a pleasure outing. These are treacherous seas, and a storm can blow up out of nowhere. The storm didn't bother Jesus the landlubber, who slept on, but it terrified the fishermen, and they hurriedly woke him from his exhausted sleep, ticking him off in the process. Jesus is so matter-of-fact in his stilling of the storm that we imagine him stirring in his sleep, dealing with the wind as you would shout at a barking dog, and turning over again, leaving the disciples dumbfounded. There is no need for us to panic. Our heavenly Father has everything under control; we simply need to live in unity with him. Go back to sleep.

QUESTIONS:

At what points each day do I "cross over" from one subculture to another? Is Jesus my companion on the crossing, allowing me to bring reconciliation and understanding? Do I allow God to still the waters that trouble me?

PRAYER:

O God, when the storm comes up from nowhere, give me the sleep of a trusting child, that I may not rock the boat in my panic but remain with Jesus in unity with you by your Spirit.

Day 14 ▶

MARK 5:1–20

> *They came to Jesus and saw the demoniac sitting there, clothed and in his right mind, the very man who had had the legion; and they were afraid.*

After crossing over, Jesus arrives at the city of Gerasa and immediately finds that it is no picnic he has come to. No sooner has he stepped off the boat than he is confronted by a wild madman, the kind of nutcase you dread wandering in off the street on the very Sunday evening you've arranged a nice little service with silent prayer and Gregorian chant.

This is no ordinary madman. Mark goes into great detail describing powerfully and vividly the tragedy of this giant of a man whose tortured mind drove him to lacerate himself with sharp stones, and to terrorize the locality with his violent shrieking, which never stopped, night or day. The neighbors were at their wits' end; every attempt to contain him had failed. The police said there was nothing more they could do, while the hospital said his insurance just didn't cover it.

And yet there was loveliness in this tormented man. As soon as he saw Jesus in the distance, "he ran and bowed down before him." Oh, that a few more of his hearers had done the same! As we have already seen, when it comes to recognizing Jesus for who he really is, it is the "mad" who are way ahead of the "normal." Unlike the rest of us, they have no time or opportunity to develop a double life. They do not build up a public face to conceal an inner reality; what you see is what you get.

He also feared Jesus for what he might do. He was tormented but dreaded further torment in the furious battle that would rage within him should Jesus attempt to cleanse him. This is the tragedy of our condition whenever we are backed into a corner by sin; we are tormented souls, we cannot sleep, we cannot pray, but we dread the violent struggle that penitence and forgiveness would demand. We want God, our only hope, to go away. "I adjure you by God, do not torment me."

When Jesus asks him his name, the reply is pure pathos. It's a one-liner that sums up not only the tragedy of this man's condition but the tragedy of all human nature, trapped in a hundred and one variations on the theme of imprisonment, awaiting release and rescue: "My name is Legion; for we are many."

For each one of us, there are too many people inside struggling to get out from our divided personality: the "me" of my hopes and aspirations, the "me" that others see, the "me" of the night watches when I cannot sleep, the "me" of my finest hour, the "me" that even I cannot admit to: "My name is Legion; for we are many."

Jesus' solution is somewhat unusual and cannot be recommended in most cases. It is certainly not available from a regular HMO. Close to where Jesus and the possessed man were talking, a great herd of pigs was feeding (proof positive that we are in non-Jewish territory), and Jesus acceded to the man's request that the unclean spirits be banished into the pigs. As proof that the transfer is successfully completed, the tormented animals immediately commit suicide with a dramatic headlong dash over the cliffs into the sea.

To dream up natural explanations for such an inexplicable event always seems to me a waste of time. We just have to accept that here we enter realms of the supernatural that we cannot pretend to understand, and that at this point we are face-to-face with the mystery of God. Certainly it had its whimsical side. Although Jesus' upbringing deprived him of the joy of eating pork, and his disciples may have been glad to see the backs of these "unclean" animals, this remedy for mental illness does seem a little hard on these creatures who, two minutes before, had been happily grunting away among the acorns.

It was also a tremendous way to launch a mission in a new territory—he was interviewed on the national as well as the regional news that night. But it was hardly likely to endear him to the local branch of the Farmers' Union.

Understandably, the deprived herdsmen race back to town to raise the alarm. The locals hurry over to see what had happened, and are amazed to find this notorious lunatic there in his best blue jeans and crisp white T-shirt, sitting on a wall, chatting quietly with Jesus. The crowd is astonished and afraid. This is all too much for them; there are things happening here that are deeply disturbing. In a rather restrained fashion, considering what havoc Jesus has caused to the local economy, they respectfully ask that Jesus moves along. Just like the rest of us when God gets too close for comfort, they "beg Jesus to leave their neighborhood."

QUESTIONS:
In what areas of my life do I fear God is getting too close for comfort? At what point do I ask Jesus to "move along"?

PRAYER:
O God, rescue me from the prisons I create for myself, that clothed by your Spirit with the mind of Christ, I may be at peace with you and with myself.

Day 15 ▸

MARK 5:21–43

He took her by the hand and said to her, "Talitha cum," which means, "Little girl, get up!"

Jesus takes the hint, tells his disciples to pack their bags, and retraces his steps to the other side of the lake. On landing he is once again immediately surrounded by "a great crowd," and is thrust into another crisis, this time at the heart of the Jewish establishment. Having dealt with a pagan madman whom no one would admit to being related to, he now finds himself dealing with a ruler of the local synagogue whose little daughter is gravely ill. In a short distance, Jesus travels from one end of the socioreligious spectrum to the other.

Jairus suffers from none of the doubts that later assailed the Jewish authorities—Jesus is the man; he will do it. However snooty some Jewish leaders were about this sensationalist maverick prophet, here was a synagogue official going down on bended knee to implore his help. When the life of someone we love is in peril, we will stop at nothing to save them. Jairus has his priorities right: life before sound doctrine and piety.

Interestingly it is others—the busybodies and the professionals—who throw cold water on this embarrassing attempt to drag in the wonder worker. They seem to dismiss Jairus as a pathetic, doting father who has taken leave of his senses; they will sort things out without any help from an upstart preacher from Nazareth of all places.

Before Jesus has even reached Jairus' house, an interfering neighbor takes over and heartlessly announces that the girl is dead and that Jesus can be told "not today, thank you." When he presses on, the professional mourners, their commission at stake, laugh their heads off at Jesus' assertion that the dead girl is only sleeping.

Jesus stands for no nonsense here and has all the hangers-on put out of the house (how Peter and the "Sons of Thunder" must have enjoyed their newfound role as club bouncers, man-handling those burly, caterwauling friends and relations onto the pavement!). Only the girl's parents and close family are left as Jesus brings the girl back to life in a scene of great tenderness. His final instruction to give her something to eat (no doubt a soft-boiled egg with hot buttered toast) is one of those delightful, realistic touches that suffuse the Gospel with total authenticity.

The walk to Jairus' house is of course "interrupted" by the incident of the woman with a hemorrhage.

Dropping to the bottom end of the social scale, here is a woman who feels that she dare not address the great Teacher directly, but who is sure that if she can even just touch the clothes he is wearing, all shall be well. Financially impoverished through her reliance on physicians (Mark seems to relish that point—do we get the impression that he and Doctor Luke were not bosom pals?), this woman was rich in faith.

When she makes contact, Jesus senses that "power had gone forth from him," and Mark records that amazingly cheeky retort (v. 31) of his very stupid disciples. They of course were much too busy swaggering about as minders (and pretty hopeless ones) to see the significance of Jesus' sense of diminution. He is like a great reservoir of God's energy and love, from which those in need draw that water without which there can be no life or hope. Each healing act contributes to the slow depletion of his reserves until, on the cross, he is drained and emptied completely. In the Resurrection he is not merely replenished to overflowing, but lost in the great unfathomable sea of God's inexhaustible love.

QUESTION:

Do I ever pour cold water—as a professional or as a busybody—upon God's initiatives to bring healing and reconciliation to a sick, broken world?

PRAYER:

O God, however great my poverty, make me rich in faith, that by your Spirit I may take hold of Jesus' garment and be healed.

Day 16 ▶

MARK 6:1–6

And they took offense at him.

These six verses give us a marvelous insight into the capricious-ness of human nature, as well as reinforcing again the sense of natural authenticity in Mark's account. A smoother operator than Mark would have hushed up this unseemly episode, but his irrepressible childlike approach ensures that everything comes out just as it happened. Jesus, fresh from sensational ex-ploits throughout Galilee and beyond, having been idolized by record crowds every step of the way, returns to his hometown. Our first stab at writing the script would give him a hero's wel-come: a banner strung across Main Street reading "Welcome Home, Nazareth's Hero," a tour of the town in a convertible, and a reception at City Hall.

But we would be miles off course with that scenario. What do our petty, jealous little minds enjoy more than having a go at someone who has made it in the world but who we knew as a little boy down our street? Why should it all hap-pen for him? Who does he think he is anyway? His family is no better than yours or mine! For every *This Is Your Life* pro-gram full of warm, tearful reunions of celebrities and their long-lost friends, there are a dozen "Former bodyguard re-veals all" demolition jobs from aggrieved acquaintances and former associates eager to get in on the act. Had Judas not committed suicide, he could have made a fortune with the tabloid press.

So even in the case of Jesus, who was love, who was transparent with the goodness of God, who had spent himself for his people, the rules and regulations of depraved humanity run their course. The Sunday congregation was not at all impressed with this local boy made good. Never mind what he was saying, or doing; they knew him, had known him from the time he was a mere kid; from where did he get all this theological gobbledygook, these high-and-mighty ways? Why, his mother takes in washing, his brothers hang out on the wrong side of the tracks, and his sisters are no better than they should be! Just who does he think he is? He may pull the wool over people's eyes at Capernaum, but he won't fool us! "And they took offense at him."

We cannot be surprised if Jesus was distressed. He had looked forward so much to coming back home; it was to have been such a special time of grace. His mother had been busy spring cleaning and baking his favorite cakes, the family had moved all the beds around to give him a room on his own, and his brothers had hired the hotel's function room for a really good bash. He longed to share with them all that God his father had been doing through him, to relate his adventures and narrow escapes, to worry with them about the future, to laugh with them about the funny things that had happened to him on the way to the synagogue, and (dare he say it) to have a few days' break from those dumbo disciples.

The naked hostility of these people whom he had known from childhood hit him hard. How could they do it? Not just to him, but to themselves, for they were fouling their own nests, tearing up the ticket that would carry them away from this mess they called daily life. How could they be so prejudiced and blind as to reject him with such contempt? "He was amazed at their unbelief." Jesus is not derailed. He ministers to those who would listen and who had grace enough to ask for help, but this rejection is a bitter blow. After weeks and months of continuous, rapturous applause, he is suddenly booed off the stage. And not in some one-horse town in the back of beyond but of all places here, his own hometown, which he had always loved and defended, even though it was the butt of every stand-up comic throughout the night clubs of Israel.

The second part of verse 6 is the saddest of all. Feeling he has been drummed out of town, he slinks away to the little villages surrounding Nazareth. These are nowhere places where he must labor in humiliating circumstances. Like a Chinese university professor forced, in the Cultural Revolution, to wring the necks of chickens all day and every day in some remote rural backwater, Jesus experiences what it means to be an outcast.

This incident at Nazareth doesn't set him back for long, but it brings him up with a start. This is just a foretaste of what is to come. The road he must travel is not going to be lined with cheering crowds all the way. Sooner or later they will turn nasty. The route on from Nazareth leads directly to Golgotha. The die is cast. There is no escape from the will of God.

QUESTION:

When does my own pride and prejudice prevent me from hearing the lifesaving words of God?

PRAYER:

O God, when the crowd turns on me and I feel as alone as Jesus did, may your Spirit show me that I too am your child, and that peace lies in doing your will.

Day 17 ►

MARK 6:7–44

He called the twelve and began to send them out two by two,
and gave them authority over the unclean spirits. . . . But he
answered them, "You give them something to eat."

There's nothing like a fresh initiative to get the adrenaline
going after a setback, and the incident at Nazareth is soon reduced in Jesus' mind to a little local difficulty as he inaugurates
a significant new phase in his campaign with the commissioning of his twelve closest followers as "officers" in his little
revolutionary army of the love of God. The sending out of
the twelve is remarkably tightly organized and precise; there
is no fuzziness or indecision. Every eventuality is catered for
in a well-thought-out operation that would have done a military commander proud. It is, however, an exceptionally tough
assignment, and this point can be said to mark the disciples'
coming of age. They now know just what they have let themselves in for; the days of strutting around self-importantly at
the head of Jesus' procession are gone for good. To rub the
message in, news has just come through of the horrific death
of John, who prepared the way for Jesus and in due course for
themselves. As Dietrich Bonhoeffer put it, "When Christ calls
a person, he bids them come and die."

Like police officers patrolling the rough side of one of our
cities, they will go out in pairs, but they are to travel light, with
an absolute minimum of gear (certainly no two-way radio) and
no food or money at all. They are to live entirely off the land,
relying on the generosity of those who hear them. But this is

no cozy arrangement with some nice respectable families living in houses with two-car garages, or a special deal with a national chain of bed-and-breakfast establishments that Jesus had fixed up beforehand. No, the entry of the disciples into any town is to be seen as a symbolic prophetic act, which will bring either blessing or judgment on its inhabitants. There is nothing proper or polite about the procedure. They are simply to descend on a town, a village, or a household; set out their stall; and see who turns up. Wherever they are not received, the twelve must shake the dust off their feet in a gesture every bit as rude as the proverbial "finger" and with consequences far more momentous. Those who slam the door will have to await a new opportunity to hear the lifesaving word. For now, though, the disciples must move on.

The good news is that, at the hands of the twelve, the authority of Jesus over unclean spirits is to be extended to the four corners of the land. The disciples themselves are, as it were, extensions of Jesus' own body, moving through the territory, speaking, announcing, touching, healing. If Pentecost is the birthday of the Church, then the commissioning of the twelve is its conception. Here already in place is the mechanism by which each person who comes wholly to belong to Jesus is refashioned as an *alter Christus*, "another Christ," to extend his work through time and space until the end of creation. The Holy Spirit will breathe new life into this mechanism, and St. Paul will spell it out for us theologically when he comes to write his letters to the church at Corinth, but the concept is formed. Everything is now in place.

This concept of extension is continued when the disciples return from their first successful sortie. They come back exhilarated by this first experience of mission in the power of Jesus their master, but when he challenges them to apply their newfound power in different circumstances, they fail to make the connection.

Exhausted by their weeks in the field, the disciples are invited by Jesus to come away with him to the diocesan retreat house for a while, to rest and refresh themselves and to get some super-sized cooked breakfasts inside them.

Unfortunately the crowd gets wind of it and, knowing all the short cuts, are there to greet them on arrival! Jesus cannot get cross with them; they are such eager beavers, so anxious to know more, and so lost and leaderless, so vulnerable. He has no option but to settle down to another bout of teaching, his disciples alongside him.

After a daylong session, the weary disciples have had enough. They ostentatiously look at their watches, shuffle about in their seats, and follow up any diversion they can think of. In the end, concern for the crowd's welfare seems the best way to bring their tireless teacher to his senses. The crowd must be ravenous by now, and the twelve suggest he says the closing prayer forthwith and sends the people off to get a meal.

Jesus immediately throws the matter back in their court; they must stop looking to others to bail them out. They have the key: "*You* give them something to eat." Still they talk of going off to buy provisions (in a question not entirely devoid of former impertinence), always looking for answers from outside. But Jesus patiently instructs them by recalling them always to themselves and to the resources at their disposal. However meager they seem, they are sufficient for God. There is no need to look elsewhere. God has given us everything we need.

QUESTION:
When do I try and shift onto others responsibility for the things God wants me to undertake with my own resources?

PRAYER:

O God, by the power of your Spirit, may my hands be the hands of Jesus, bringing to the world your blessing and peace.

Day 18 ▶

MARK 6:45–56

"Take heart, it is I; do not be afraid."

Another "immediately," another crossing over, as Jesus withdraws with his disciples to the other side of the lake for another attempt to gain respite from the crowd. This time Jesus gets the disciples to drop him off at a secluded cove so that he can escape into the hills to pray. They remain a little way out to sea, and enjoy a picnic lunch, lounging on deck and swimming from the boat. As he prays, Jesus is conscious of their laughter in the distance. The disciples grow careless, fail to watch for signs of changing weather conditions, and suddenly find themselves struggling against an adverse wind, their oars making little headway.

Jesus, though deep in prayer, does not shut himself off from them, and soon becomes aware of their distress. Again, as in the previous crossing, he reestablishes order and peace, rescuing them from their panic. This time they see him walking from the shore across the surface of the sea, and initially they are more terrified than ever. But Jesus identifies himself, reassures them, and climbs aboard. The image of Jesus getting into the same boat as the disciples (when, Mark notes, "he meant to pass them by") is a powerful picture of his coming alongside us in our predicament of human experience. He may like to think he means to pass us by, but he finds he cannot. His compassion always gets the better of him, whatever the risks.

Kenneth Cragg calls Jesus "the signature of God." We all know God is love, but just like that job offer, we need to get it in writing! Jesus is he who himself signs the new agreement between God and humanity. At Jesus' hands, torn by the nails, God guarantees to deliver that peace which is beyond understanding and that joy which no one can ever take from us. Our part of the agreement is simply to open our hearts to surrender ourselves to all that God longs to share with us. Only in this way are we able to face with courage and composure everything that life can throw at us. In the words of Pierre Teilhard de Chardin:

> To the hands that broke and gave life to the bread,
> that blessed and caressed, that were pierced, . . . to the
> kindly and mighty hands that reach down to the very
> marrow of the soul—that mould and create—to the
> hands through which so great a love is transmitted—it
> is to these hands that it is good to surrender our soul.

The disciples' hearts, however, were not yet open wide enough. It was premature to talk of surrender. Mark links their astonishment at Jesus' coming to them on the water with their failure to understand what he had been doing when he fed the crowd with the meager resources of five loaves and two fish. "Their hearts were hardened." Despite their exciting experiences in the mission field, they are soon fearful and downcast, soon thrown off course. Their dull minds run on rail lines, limiting God's activity to particular areas of life, confining him to tested and approved methods, cutting him down to their size. Their God is too small. They want him to keep regular hours whereas, as John Donne reminds us (in his sermon "Mercies of God"), God is never constrained by our narrow, restrictive practices: "We ask *'panem quotidianum,'* our daily bread, and God never says you should have come yesterday, he never says you must come again tomorrow, but today if you will hear his voice, today he will hear you." On landfall they were again besieged by crowds desperate for healing and help. Evidently news of the woman with the hemorrhage had traveled fast, and we see yet another variation on the extension of Jesus' ministry. Now it was no longer necessary for Jesus to touch them; they had only to "touch even the fringe of his cloak" for all to be well. Once the power of God is released, there is no end, no limit, to his work of healing and reconciliation. In the divine chemical reaction between the power of God and the faith of the believer, no channel of grace is left unused, no disciple's hands need be idle.

QUESTION:

Have I failed to make the connection between all that God has done for me and all that God intends to do, in different ways and with different methods?

PRAYER:

O God, in Jesus you come among us where we are and as we are. Help us by your Spirit no longer to be afraid, but to place ourselves wholly in your perfect will.

Day 19 ▶

MARK 7:1–23

"You have a fine way of rejecting the commandment of God in order to keep your tradition!"

Those called to the married state will know all about our uncanny ability to notice straightaway, not the things our loved one has managed to get done but the one thing left undone. An hour generously donated (or so we feel) to cleaning up the kitchen may well evoke the response, "I thought you might have emptied the dishwasher."

The Pharisees were very interested in dish washing; so much so that when they arrive to quiz Jesus, backed up by some whiz-kid scribes (all cell phones and Gucci shoes) driven in by limo from the city for the weekend, they immediately "noticed that some of his disciples were eating with defiled hands, that is, without washing them." Never mind his message, his healings, his feedings, his celebration of God; they can get him on a technicality.

Watch out! We are all constantly in danger here. Jesus' quoting of Isaiah 29:13 is meant for us today just as much as for the Pharisees, and we have less excuse. It is so easy to pay him mere lip service, and to allow our quaint customs to get in the way of God.

Every parish community I have worked in has been rebuilt on weekends away when, free from the pressures of home routine, we have grown together into a deeper sense of union with God. On some of those weekends we made the Sunday Eucharist an all-day affair; the ministry of the word before coffee, the ministry of the sacrament before lunch, and the post-Communion reflection before a final snack. One hiccup when this manner of worship was first proposed was the worry about fasting before Communion: How could we have pastries and coffee and then go straight to the altar for the sacrament? Fortunately it didn't take us too long to work out that the celebration of God embracing our whole day could not be jeopardized by an attachment to a relic of early morning Communion. Fasting is good; but encountering the Lord in a new way is even better.

We can see the beauty of the Pharisees' system of course when, on our way to church, we are flagged down by the driver of a car in trouble. How convenient to feel absolved of further responsibility because we are on God's business and cannot stop. "'Whatever support you might have had from me is Corban' (that is, an offering to God)."

"Corban" comes in very handy inside church too. Most of us who have been at this Christianity lark for some time were brought up with strict rules about how to behave on our way to and from the altar. Our gaze was to be religiously restricted to the grating in the floor; eye contact with any other living creature was definitely taboo. How much more so at the moment of Communion itself; God forbid that we should look at one another! All our smiles were to be "Corban"—"'thus making void the word of God through your tradition that you have handed on.'"

"In presenting the bread or cup, it is essential that there be a personal moment, a meeting of eyes when one says 'The body of Christ' and the other affirms 'Amen.'" So writes the American liturgist Gabe Huck in articulating the mind of the Church on contemporary liturgy renewed by the Spirit. The Spirit of God has brought us a long way in a short time and revealed to us that it is no longer a case of either-or. We can honor the Real Presence of Christ in the Eucharist and at the same time honor His Presence in the assembly of the faithful, in one another. At the altar of God, a loving smile, a spoken name is no longer "Corban," for we are *all* "Corban"—an offering to God—we are all his holy, priestly people.

Having sorted that one out, Jesus turns to deal with that other fallacy kept alive by the religious establishment: that defilement is a matter of external contamination. Nonsense of course, because it all depends on what's inside us in the first place.

The two sweet and very devout old ladies I encountered in my Northamptonshire days, who misused the adjective *fornicating* with happy abandon (as in "Fornicating weather for this time of year, Father"), could do so in utter innocence precisely because "to the pure all things are pure."

Jesus knew that the reverse is equally true. Where sin is concerned, there's no need to launch a police investigation; it's always an inside job.

QUESTION:
In what way are my own religious customs inhibiting my encounter—or the encounter of others—with the living God?

PRAYER:
O God, by your life-giving Spirit, teach me to delight in others that I may honor you, and to follow those whose example helps me to be like Jesus.

Day 20 ▶

MARK 7:24–37

"For saying that, you may go—the demon has left your daughter."

Another day off, and this time Jesus really tries to get away from it all with a special round-trip deal to Tyre and Sidon, about as far away as he could get from his home territory. There he lies low at the house of a friend of a friend, but to no avail, for "he could not escape notice."

The interruption comes in a form doubly disturbing to Jesus. Not only is he cheated of his desperately needed solitude, but the person who invades his privacy and demands his help is (to them) a mere woman, and a foreigner at that. Ched Myers identifies this request as an "affront to the honor status of Jesus," and the rebuff she receives, although it can have come as no surprise, is startling in its severity. Jesus apparently loses his cool and, in likening non-Jews to "dogs," he expresses an attitude toward outsiders that would have raised a cheer among the rednecks in the bars of Nazareth.

The woman's riposte adds insult to injury, but wins the day. Jesus suddenly switches track, accedes to her request, and announces that her daughter is healed. Jesus does so, *not* because of her faith, but because of her quick and witty repartee. He who outwitted the Pharisees every time admits that this woman, this outsider, has got the better of him. He allows himself to be "shamed" in this way in order to include this pagan woman in the new community of the Kingdom.

Like Jacob (Genesis, chapter 32), this woman wrestles with God and prevails. Jacob was given a new name by which God's people are to be known: Israel or "he who struggles with God." Unknowingly she stumbles upon the secret of the Kingdom of God and, in her lively knockabout with the Lord's Anointed, enters into his realm. As Izaak Walton wrote of John Donne: "God wrestled with him . . . and marked him; marked him for his own."

For anyone who, like me, would move heaven and earth to get out of gym class, Tertullian has some bad news: "We may wrestle with him in our supplications, for this violence God delights in."

On my arrival as the new parish priest of a Yorkshire church, I was confronted by a warning sign in the sacristy that read, "The Peace is not shared in this church." How ironic that it is

MARK MY WORD ◂ 57

often those who pride themselves on being sacramentalists who nurse a deep-seated suspicion of any form of tactile ministry.

Jesus puts us straight with a highly tactile and unseemly bit of prodding and poking of the deaf man with a speech impediment. Here again the Jewish purity code, not to mention our sense of what is decent, is knocked out of the ring, for Jesus uses saliva in this healing when in the Jewish world it was considered as strong a pollution as excrement (Leviticus 15:8).

All this made the crowds "astounded beyond measure," and we need to awaken again our sense of awe at all that God is doing in breaking down the barriers that separate us from him. In our liturgies and in our spiritual formation, we are now well aware of the need to create a place where the loving, gentle touch of God is known, but a sense of awe is equally important.

Archbishop Laud found it necessary in the seventeenth century to comment that "it is called superstition nowadays for any man to come with more reverence into a church than a tinker and his dog into an ale-house." Before we get too cozy with God, leaning with our elbows on the altar table as we sip our after-service coffee, let's hear again the word of God speaking through the "golden-mouthed" St. John Chrysostom, who reminds us that, for Christians with eyes to see, the altar will always be "a place of shuddering and terror."

QUESTION:

Am I wrestling with God in a real encounter, or am I always asking for a note to be excused from gym class?

PRAYER:

O God, by your Spirit, touch me, handle me, wrestle with me as you will, so that I may be marked forever as your own, through Jesus who bears the marks of the nails.

Day 21 ▸

MARK 8:1–21

He asked them, "How many loaves do you have?"

For Jesus this was a bad day. True, it started out all right, the plight of the crowd finding a ready response in his big heart, but it wasn't long before the disciples were up to their old tricks, and by evening he could cheerfully have wrung their necks.

It was only a short time previously that the disciples had been party to the feeding of a large crowd, but they display very short memories. On that occasion they had been indignant at the thought that anything could be done, cheekily answering back their leader (Mark 6:37), and this time they simply lapse into despair, wimps to a man. Not long after being ordained, I was given responsibility one year for the parish's summer camp on the Isle of Wight. I still remember a sermon on this passage preached in a little country church nearby, "explaining away" the miracle as a bit of social engineering. All the people in the crowd would have had something up their sleeve; they just needed a signal to start sharing it around.

At the time, as an overzealous curate, I expressed concern at having exposed my flock to a dangerous dose of liberalism, but now I see the preacher was on to something. The intervention of Jesus remains the crucial thing, and as always when working on us, he presses the button that releases what is already within us. There was no need for him to fly-in four thousand prepacked lunches on plastic trays; the resources were all on site, and needed only to be released.

Our world is full of food, but people go hungry. Congregations are full of money, but people won't get it out of their pockets. Human beings are capable of living life just a little lower than the angels, but we prefer captivity on little treadmills of our own devising. We need Jesus to call for hush, to take a loaf, and to show how life is to be lived.

A faith community can cling to life indefinitely on a life-support machine or, through the energy of the Spirit, it can experience dramatic recovery. The individuals concerned are precisely the same people as before, but they have been transformed, and their gifts and ministries (hidden up very long sleeves) released for all to enjoy and to benefit from. A stewardship campaign doesn't make new money; it simply releases what has been there all the time. "How many loaves do you have?" is always the first question Jesus asks. He wants us to focus on what raw materials we have in our hand, what is at our disposal and under our control. If we offer him that, we can leave the rest to him. Never mind what we used to have, or wish we had, or what others have; he can do everything he wants to do using only what we happen to be holding in our hand. Offering him our "loaf" without question enables him to operate the release mechanism for the crowd around us. As Mother Teresa said, "We are not called to do great things, only little things with great love."

Only later does the day begin to go wrong for Jesus. First the Pharisees with more tests and trick questions, their hearts baked hard in the religious furnace that was Palestine. That Jesus "sighed deeply in his spirit" gives us only a glimpse of his frequent moments of despair and exasperation at his inability to get through to them.

He is glad to get away from them and to be alone in the boat with his friends. Here it gets even worse. Jesus wasn't feeling at his best, and as soon as he attempts to teach them the significance of what he has been doing in relation to political events that will soon engulf them, they sit at the other end of the boat muttering to themselves about having brought only one loaf for their supper.

This marks the low point in his relationship with them throughout his ministry, and he blasts them out of the water with a tirade of stinging intensity (vv. 17–21). The disciples themselves, the very ones Jesus had counted on, are guilty of the stubbornness warned of by Isaiah and quoted previously by Jesus (Mark 4:12) in relation to "those outside."

As Snoopy would say, one can only go to bed and hope tomorrow will be a better day.

QUESTIONS:
What gift do I tend to keep hidden up my sleeve? Isn't it about time I allowed it to be used by God for the benefit of my community?

PRAYER:
O God, when you ask, "How many loaves do you have?" help me to offer you what I kept hidden, knowing that, in the power of your Spirit, what I have is all you need to transform the world through Jesus, who releases us.

Day 22 ▶

MARK 8:22—9:1

Then Jesus laid his hands on his eyes again.

Again is the most significant little word in this passage. What on earth is going on here? Jesus apparently cannot hack it. He has to have two goes at a simple little healing project.

Mark paints the scene in touching detail. Jesus is moved by the plight of this blind man—no beggar, but someone blessed with true friends who did not simply deliver him to Jesus and dump him in the queue but intervened on his behalf. Like kind hosts in a foreign country who know how to handle the local bureaucracy, they do more than tell you the way; they go down to the office with you, bang on the counter, and even, *in extremis,* slip the official the requisite number of dollar bills.

The friends' efforts are rewarded; Jesus listens and immediately sets about processing their application. As usual there's a hullabaloo going on around them, so Jesus takes the blind man by the hand and personally escorts him outside the village to a quiet spot where they could be alone. Throwing conventional purity laws to the wind, Jesus spits on the man's eyes, lays his hands on him, and inquires with a kindly bedside manner whether the circles are clearer on the red or the green background.

The man sees, but the image is blurred. As with the rest of us having our eyes tested, it always seems impossible to say whether adding that particular lens helps or not. The optometrist must simply plod on, gritting his teeth as he says with studied patience, "Let's try that one again, shall we?"

Likewise for this new patient, Jesus has to do it again, and this for us is part of the good news. Our new life centered on God will not often be the case of a quick answer or immediate results. We will have to go back to the starting block again and again; we shall sometimes despair of ourselves, disappoint those who expect much from us, and look foolish in front of those who stand and gape. If the Christian life is process not event, we will need to begin again, many times.

What happens next is more striking still; Jesus gets something wrong. After he has sent the man on his way rejoicing, Jesus first hammers home in deed and word his central theme of reversal as one of the keys of the Kingdom. Peter takes a nose dive from prospective "prince of the Church" to "Satan" quicker than a futures trader on the stock exchange, and the whole bunch are reminded in no uncertain terms that if they are going to get anywhere with God, they are in for some heavy short-term losses. At the end of this crescendo on reversal, he asserts that the Kingdom of God will "come with power" within the lifetime of at least some of his hearers.

Eschatological prophecy does not appear to have been his strong point. Subsequent events of history proved Jesus wrong, and we are left wishing he had simply kept off the subject. Or are we? Perhaps rather we should be extremely grateful to God that occasionally Jesus wandered off into areas in which he managed to get a few wires crossed.

Just how many Christians, I wonder, have we lost overboard through the Church's laggardly coming clean on the limitations of Jesus' knowledge? There must be a whole lost tribe of ex–Sunday school pupils out there, wandering in the wilderness, because they think that in order to accept Jesus as the life-transforming power of their lives, they would be required to believe that this first-century Jew from a small town in Galilee walked around equipped with a divine computer instead of a human brain. No, occasionally Jesus got it wrong, thank God; he really was one of us after all.

QUESTIONS:

Do the struggles and limitations of Jesus worry or disturb us in our spiritual journey? Or do they release us from the impossible demands of previous generations and distant cultures?

PRAYER:

O God, may I rejoice in the struggles of Jesus and make them mine as, amid the limitations of our human condition, I commit myself into your loving hands.

Day 23 ▶

MARK 9:2-32

"This kind can come out only through prayer."

At a high school in England, where selected senior students are appointed as "prefects" to share disciplinary duties with the teaching staff, I was at that time too short and skinny to be considered suitable. Eventually, having eaten enough dumplings by then, I was admitted to that charmed circle of minor gods who wore gold braid on their school uniform. The moment was all the sweeter for the delay, and I was soon dismissing the whole school after assembly as tyrannically as the biggest and best of them.

Jesus appointed three prefects—Peter and the two Zebedee boys—and they took themselves very seriously indeed. Every so often Jesus would organize an in-service training day for them, and one such day was the time he took them mountain walking (hopefully with a can of grapefruit segments, but early texts are unclear).

Predictably the three big shots were full of themselves, issuing many orders to the nine riffraff about cleaning up the camp while they were gone, but before very long it was clear that Peter, James, and John had bitten off more than they could chew.

On the mountain they were caught up in a vision of a kind they had only heard about in their Bible class at synagogue. The sort of thing that happened to Moses or Elijah was happening to them! This was one in the eye for that snooty rabbi who had written on Peter's school report "tries hard but short concentration span makes further progress unlikely." These three local boys made (fairly) good, none of them very bright, saw things on this day that were quite beyond them, things they would only begin to understand when Jesus had gone and when the pieces of the puzzle began to fall into place. As Peter himself was to write later (or so he claimed—the others thought he had to find someone to ghost it for him), these events were "things into which angels long to look" (1 Peter 1:12).

That was later. Right now Peter, as if to confirm his rabbi's worst suspicions, immediately began making a fool of himself, coming up with some crazy idea of building restrooms for the spiritual VIPs. But to be fair, they were all frightened out of their wits.

In the middle of it all, out of the cloud, comes that voice, the voice that some of them had heard (it seems an age ago) on the banks of the Jordan, confirming this mystery man as "beloved Son" of God. Suddenly, the Sinai experience—the leaders of the chosen people communing with God on the mountaintop—an experience they had until then merely heard about in synagogue, is now *their* experience. God is no longer secondhand.

They were exhilarated and they were humbled by what had happened to them, but as they began the descent, emerging from the mist into the sunlight, some of their old bravado returned. They began to congratulate one another on being selected for this top-secret special mission, and James and John promised not to tell the others about Peter's crazy idea. There was a swagger in their step as they neared base camp, and they sincerely hoped those other layabouts had the coffeepot on.

They were to be disappointed, although not as much as Jesus. The other nine, left to themselves for just a few hours, had become embroiled in a fracas with the scribes, and a large crowd had gathered to see the fun. Evidently it had all started when a local man, at his wits' end with worry about his epileptic son, had brought him to the disciples, who were able to do nothing for him. Jesus is not well pleased.

In telling the sick boy's father to believe and the hapless disciples to pray, he is saying the same thing. Whether victim or helper, we need simply to live in unity with God our Father in order that our prayers may be answered and his power released in us.

A lot of trouble has come from our seeing "belief" as a struggle to keep up with Jesus or the doctrines of the Church or the conventional wisdom of established Christianity, as we fall further and further behind, despairing and out of breath. Marcus Borg points out that in both Greek and Latin, the roots of "to believe" mean "to give one's heart to." Much to our relief therefore, we find that "believing in Jesus does not mean believing doctrines about him. Rather, it means to give one's heart, one's self at its deepest level, to the post-Easter Jesus who is the living Lord."

QUESTION:

Do we believe that "all things are possible" to those who give their hearts to God?

PRAYER:

O God, teach us to pray that we may enjoy such unity with you that we may drive out the darkness and bring in your Kingdom, through Jesus who in the Spirit was one with you.

Day 24 ▸

MARK 9:30–50

They went on from there.

Jesus' day out with his leadership team had turned sour. In the space of an hour or two, he had passed from the blinding light of the mountaintop experience of God to the daily grind of life with the twelve. Elation had given way to despair as he strove to open the minds and gird the wills of these strugglers.

It was not just a question of repeatedly failing their field-work tests—basic proficiency would come with time—but they had no grasp of theory. They seemed to have a very tenuous hold on the reality of the situation, not realizing that they were engaged in a desperate confrontation with all the powers that held back humankind from knowing God. This struggle must inevitably lead to death, not just for Jesus, but for all but one of these men who now argued with each other about the seating plan around the boardroom table. When he tried to drum some sense into their heads with some straight talking, they stare at their shoes for a moment and then change the subject.

The basic problem with the disciples was that they thought they had arrived, whereas they had only just begun. They were pleased as punch to have been selected by this sensational teacher as members of his inner circle. Although life on the road had its drawbacks, it certainly beat the fishing industry as a way of life. They were enjoying what perks had already come their way, and were busy looking forward to goodies that were bound to follow once their leader was in control of the country. Only gradually, and with great reluctance, were they realizing that Jesus had a different agenda: that the normal pecking order was to be reversed; that in the new Kingdom of God, the child was to be the model of greatness; that all their jostling for position had been an utter waste of time—indeed it had put them right at the bottom of the pile.

The other lesson they were just beginning to get hold of was that their being on the road was not only a necessary means of disseminating a message but was in itself a parable of the journey they had begun from self to God.

That journey, begun by twelve men during the hot summer of the year 30, is continued by all who seek God and attempt to place their feet in the footmarks of Jesus the Christ. At various stages in the journey we can be tempted to imagine that we have arrived; Confirmation can become a commencement celebration with no intention of active service ahead; release of the Spirit can lead us into a self-indulgent heavenly trance of no earthly use to anyone; ordination can be reduced to a meal ticket for life. We have arrived; we have earned a rest. The current emphasis on "being" rather than "doing" has been a necessary corrective to frenzied activity and anxious Christian living, but it should never fool us into thinking we have made it.

Lest we should be in any doubt about this, Jesus delivers a broadside to the disciples on the question of accountability and judgment. The renewal movement has quite rightly brought God in from the cold to sit alongside us around the hearth, but the result is that we now find it more difficult to take seriously the dire warnings of Jesus.

Jesus looks through outward appearances into the hearts of his people, lost and leaderless, and the depth of his compassion for them explains the fierceness of his language when describing the fate of anyone who leads them away from the path toward the Kingdom. Those ordained in the days of the old Prayer Book will recall the echo of that warning enshrined in those awesome words spoken by the bishop, "Ye know the greatness of the fault, and also the horrible punishment that shall ensue."

We must reserve our greatest severity for ourselves, and Jesus launches into some of his most colorful hyperbole in making sure the disciples realize that amputation is preferable to knocking at the gates of hell with all our limbs and organs in sound working order. The calling to be a follower of Jesus calls for naked ruthlessness, and we had better be ready.

The disciple, like best back bacon, acquires flavor and purpose by being cooked until crisp, "for everyone will be salted with fire."

QUESTIONS:

In what ways do we think we have arrived with God? Have we sat down for a rest, believing the journey is for the most part behind us?

PRAYER:

O God, may we see with your eyes your little ones, and by your Spirit, accept the need for their sake to be salted with fire as Jesus was.

Day 25 ▸

MARK 10:1–16

"Whoever divorces his wife and marries another commits adultery against her."

What a loser! Jesus' insistence on a total prohibition on divorce was not good news for the PR department. "Boss, this will never win us votes!" The boss took no notice; indeed he toughened his stance, knowing that here he touched upon a true basic of the "new deal" with God and with each other (the one "basic" of course that politicians studiously avoid calling us back to!).

Matthew's version of the party manifesto is reasonable on this issue, seeing the matter from a male point of view, given that in contemporary Jewish society only the husband could effect a divorce. Mark's version shows Jesus in a totally unreasonable mood, extending the prohibition to apply to women as well as to men.

We should not imagine that this is a problem for our society alone. John Meier reminds us that Jesus' views on divorce reveal his marginality as a teacher in that they were a departure from "the views and practices of the major Jewish religious groups of his day." Further, the very rawness of such teaching forms the basis of the primary "criterion of discontinuity" by which New Testament scholars attempt to identify the original teaching of Jesus himself, quarried from the variety of sources (oral tradition and the evangelist's own "angle" on things) evident in the Gospels in the form they come down to us. Precisely because Jesus' teaching on divorce is discontinuous, dissimilar, and original, we can include it with some confidence in the material coming direct from the boss himself.

A further criterion used by scholars to identify original Gospel material is that of "embarrassment"—sayings of Jesus that are so embarrassing to our ears that the Church couldn't possibly have invented them! In our Western materialistic culture, Jesus' teaching on divorce wins the gold medal in the embarrassment stakes every time, and it's not just politicians who have red faces, but clergy too.

Yes, it is annoying, but Jesus knows what he is talking about. He teaches these things, not because he wants to bind and restrict us with rules, but because he wants the best for us. He knows there is no human situation, no intimate relationship that cannot be redeemed by the love of God. For those who try to live in unity with our Father are graced with the love to live in unity with all creation (even our own families!).

Of course there will be times when, because of cruelty or repeated infidelity, a spouse may in the end have no alternative but to withdraw from the marriage. This is not the same as scheming to make a divorce inevitable or seeking consolation with someone else or trading in one's partner for a newer model. Should a marriage eventually fall apart despite every effort to make it work, sustained over a long period, then there are worse horrors in life than living in the celibate state.

As ever, the teaching of Jesus is sanctified common sense, a way that ensures our lasting happiness and contentment but that we seem determined to ignore.

The most insidious and destructive idol of the twentieth century has been that of freedom of choice, the demanding as a right the freedom to hedge one's bets so that no action ever has consequences attached to it. This notion of freedom of choice actually involves never making a choice at all, but keeping our options open in an infinite number of nondecisions designed to evade taking final responsibility for our own lives and actions. Like women officers who become pregnant who sue the military for unfair dismissal, we demand compensation for the consequences of decisions we ourselves have made.

Jesus' message is all about making a choice and sticking to it, with the promise that if we are faithful, he will stick with us. Because he teaches choice for the Kingdom in a manner irrevocable and unequivocal, not letting us look back for a moment once we have put our hand to the plough, he can teach the same uncompromising truth in relation to the choice of the person with whom we shall spend the rest of our life. We have ordered our main course, and it's no use wishing we'd ordered something different when our neighbor's dish arrives, no matter how tempting it looks.

Jesus teaches choice, not because it is handed down from

Sinai on a tablet of stone, but because unless we make a choice for life, we devalue the currency of our word, our promise, our vow, and our society disintegrates before our very eyes. Of course we then proceed to blame the resultant misery and violence on everyone except ourselves. Perhaps it is no accident that at the end of this session on divorce, children are brought to him for blessing. These will be the victims whenever we choose to evade the call of Jesus to lay down our life for our friend. It is to these vulnerable ones "that the kingdom of God belongs"; here are the role models of single-hearted, unquestioning love for the adults to emulate.

QUESTIONS:

In what ways do I demand to have my cake and eat it too? In what area of my life do I now need to make a definite choice?

PRAYER:

O God, teach me not to make a god of my freedom of choice, but to choose you unconditionally, and to live with the consequences, as Jesus did, by the power of your life-giving Spirit.

Day 26 ▸

MARK 10:17–31

As he was setting out . . .

This was not a good moment to bother Jesus. He was just trying to leave the house, already running late, talking aloud to himself as he checked through the list of things he needed for the meeting, patting his pockets for his car keys, and hoping desperately he would get through the door before the phone could ring. At last he had everything he could possibly need, had switched on the alarm, and was dashing for the door, when the doorbell rings and there stands a crazy guy wearing an idiotic smile asking questions about eternity!

"Good Teacher, what must I do to inherit eternal life?"

Not the best question at that precise moment.

Jesus' answer is a bit tetchy. The questioner was surely on safe ground calling this famous Teacher "good," but is demolished as quickly as the student volunteering the wrong answer to a grumpy lecturer who had had a bad night.

It seems mighty unfair to us, who know that Jesus was good. Why is he playing games with this man?

Either Jesus also had had a bad night and just couldn't face deep theology on the doorstep at that hour of the day, or quite simply, he meant what he said: "No one is good but God alone."

This one sentence takes us straight to the Jesus of Mark, the pre-Easter Jesus, unencumbered with the Christological titles heaped upon him by an adoring and grateful Church. Here is the one True Man, the only person who has ever been completely human, the suffering servant totally obedient to the Father's will, he who is transparent with the love of God.

Here we have set before us, at a critical point in Mark's narrative, the mystery that Borg identifies as "the sharp discontinuity between the historical Jesus and the Christ of Christian tradition." No cause for alarm here, but a sense of excitement that we are onto the real thing; not a creation of theologians meeting centuries later at the command of a Roman emperor who had told them the answer along with the question, but an authentic human being who is the key to the puzzle of our existence and purpose.

Mark's Jesus is burnt up with a desire to honor God in every waking moment. He has so emptied himself of self that his will has become indistinguishable from God's will. The author of the fourth Gospel was right on target when he applied to Jesus the Psalmist's words, "Zeal for your house will consume me" (John 2:17). He was eaten up by God.

And yet here was no ranting raver, no wild man down from the hills with thorns in his beard and a mad look in his eye. Jesus breathed God through normality. Normal, everyday life took on, through him, the contours of the Kingdom of God. One minute, urgent about his Father's business with no time to spare for doorstep conversations, Jesus is giving this questioner a hard time; another moment and the compassion of his humanity breaks through, "Jesus, looking at him, loved him." The sun bursts through the clouds, and suddenly there is all the time in the world. For Jesus recognizes, in the agonized questioning of this earnest young man, total and true reality. Here is a soul teetering along the tightrope between earth and heaven; he may "make it" to the platform of respectability and success, but there is still a chance he may fall into the hands of the living God.

Jesus here shows us love, love that can ask the hard question, that is willing to risk seeing the beloved walk away downcast rather than deny love with half truths and easy empty words. Leaders of church communities with a clear vision of what it means today to belong to the Body of Christ, who "talk turkey" with young parents who come asking to "have the baby baptized," are usually accused of un-Christlike rigorism. The converse is true of course: Only those who love enough can bear to ask the hard questions by which they risk losing those they have begun to love. Let's not give the name *Christlike* to a smile, a platitude, and a christening next Sunday at 4:00 p.m., no questions asked.

Jesus' hard words on the wealthy are therefore born, not out of cold theory, but out of the pain of watching his children grow up. It grieves him deeply that such a promising recruit should in the end throw it all away for a steady job with a car and a good pension, but he would rather have no confirmations this year than a gaggle of giggling twelve-year-olds. This is serious no-prisoners-taken business.

As always, entry into the Kingdom of God is revealed as a self-selection process. We may start off by imagining that God, or at least St. Peter, is in charge of the turnpike toll booth and that we must approach it as helpless petitioners armed with exactly the right change to operate the barrier. Instead Jesus shows us a different picture. We are issued with all the necessary bits and pieces to assemble at home our DIY heavenly banqueting table, but we are left completely free to leave it dismantled in its packaging, to get it out and half finish it, or to complete it with a wobbly leg. The decision is always ours; those who live by the "Sunday Styles" section will die by the "Sunday Styles" section.

QUESTION:

When did my possessions or my prospects last cause my countenance to fall when invited by God to accompany Jesus further along the road?

PRAYER:

O God, show us how, in the pattern of Jesus, we may love and ask the hard questions at the same time, especially of ourselves.

Day 27 ▸

MARK 10:32–45

. . . and Jesus was walking ahead of them.

Those who have the privilege of living in the north of England usually have too much self-respect to talk of going "up" to London. It is always "down" to London, and it always feels downhill when you're driving southward on the motorway. Not so Jerusalem. For the faithful Jew as for the nationalistic one, it was always "up" to Jerusalem, even for the country boys from the far north.

Jerusalem is God's own city, from which David ruled when kings were really kings, where Solomon staged his nonstop spectacular and built the great Temple, where prophets harangued both monarchs and mobs to die beneath a hail of stones, where all the happenings happened, and where anyone who was anybody made his name. Indeed, "glorious things are spoken of you, O city of God" (Psalm 87:3).

If Jesus had anything to say to the world, he had no choice but to go to Jerusalem. He would otherwise have been forever consigned to the margins of Jewish life, a small-time operator for the rest of his days. For Jesus it had become a case of "*this* year Jerusalem." So up he went.

So determined was Jesus to get there that he stepped out in front, walking ahead of his little band of followers. This causes them to be "amazed," as if they were more used to playing the part of pathfinder, scouting the route, kicking any snarling dogs, having a friendly word with the desk sergeant, and tracking down a nice little bed-and-breakfast place. Suddenly Jesus has quickened the pace and changed the rules. Something is up, and the disciples don't like it: "and those who followed were afraid."

Their worst suspicions were soon realized. While they breathlessly attempted to keep up with Jesus as he strode purposefully ahead, he began to spell it out. He had to go to Jerusalem, to the capital of his country, the heart of his nation, the symbol of God's people. He could not stay at the periphery forever. Sooner or later he had to face them; enter the citadel of those who had tamed God and shut him up in a scroll in a sanctuary. He had to take them on in their own corner, and he would be defeated. He also knew that God would triumph, that death cannot be the end for those who live God, those in whom God lives.

The disciples immediately change the subject, as they had done every time Jesus veered toward the uncomfortable and embarrassing subject of his own demise. This time their preoccupation with themselves reaches new heights, and the two leather-clad bikers James and John (having reluctantly left their Harley-Davidsons at home) speak up, with no apparent shame, on the subject of the seating plan at the grand reception when it is all over.

We can only hope that this bit of Mark's Gospel is unrelated chronologically to the previous few verses; that the telephone rang when Mark was just in the middle of cutting and pasting together this section of the manuscript, and that it got all out of order.

Otherwise the jump from verse 34 to verse 35 reads like something out of a sitcom specializing in black humor: a young mother makes a moving speech to her children telling them she has inoperable cancer and is going into the hospital never to reappear, and the kids' immediate response is, "Mom, tell Gary it's my turn on the Game Boy!" With equal sensitivity, James and

MARK MY WORD ◄ 77

John (evidently the theological equivalents of Mutt and Jeff) pipe up with their request for good seats not behind a pillar.

If this incident does indeed follow directly from the prophecy of destruction and resurrection, then Jesus shows remarkable restraint. Without so much as a sigh, he explains that there is more to heaven than a seating plan. Perhaps the very innocence of the brothers' request, their transparent childish wanting of the goodies in the window, lightens his load for a moment. He can only smile to himself at their ability, amid the life-and-death decisions he has to face alone, to go on living in a world that will all-too-soon come crashing down around them. They are like children waking from a deep, untroubled sleep, desperately clinging to the dreams that are slipping inexorably from them.

It must have grieved Jesus deeply, however, that as he tried to put before them the way of self-emptying, their minds were full only of privileges and perks. Their amazing question reveals just how little they have assimilated of Jesus' teaching and basic approach. As Bishop David Jenkins put it, "If God wins through in the end, he will have suffered his way through, not bashed his way through."

"You do not know what you are asking"; yes, there will be places of honor in the Kingdom of God, but they will be reserved not for "important people," but for those who have entered into the work of Jesus by reversing the natural order of this world, exhibiting true greatness by making themselves as of no importance, and taking everything that comes as a consequence of that surrender.

This is the cup and the baptism in which they are challenged by Jesus to accept initiation. In reply they assert "we are able" only because they haven't the faintest idea what Jesus is talking about and will say anything to keep on good terms with the boss. Their eyes are still firmly fixed on those reserved places with their names inscribed in exquisite calligraphy on crisp white cards.

The others are no better. Hearing James and John articulate exactly what they themselves have been wondering, they quickly get wind of the fact that Jesus is not exactly impressed and that the two brothers have suddenly slumped to the bottom of the class. The others are loud in their condemnation, eager to show the teacher that *they* haven't been naughty, but Jesus calls them over in order to include them, along with dunces James and John, in the single mass of humanity that desperately needs to heed this message: "Whoever wishes to be first among you must be slave of all."

We should never wonder why Christianity has ceased, by and large, to make inroads into Western culture. With our bishops bedecked in imperial purple, our plastic-collared priestly caste, our enthroned celebrants and hierarchical distinctions, we seem to have done everything possible to reinforce the way of the world within the Church, arrogantly casting aside this central tenet of Jesus' life and teaching. We haven't abandoned it of course; we know it is there and can answer exam questions on it, but we have emptied it of power by making it a spiritual quality instead of a practical way of life. Very ingenious.

The Lord must be saying, "Come back, James and John; all is forgiven!"

QUESTION:

When God speaks to us of defeat and suffering, do we cry "That's not fair!" or "Let us also go, that we may die with him"?

PRAYER:

O God, when we want to make ourselves important, help us to become least of all, that in losing ourselves we may find you, in Jesus our Lord.

Day 28 ▶

MARK 10:46–52

"Go; your faith has made you well."

The sign at the filling station on the outskirts of Jericho read "last gas before Jerusalem." From there it was just fifteen miles for the pilgrims before the sacred city of David was finally reached. It was therefore a good spot for beggars. They were onto a good thing with pilgrims who, with their destination almost in sight, were in the mood to be generous with those who rattled tins under their noses and pinned flowers on their lapels.

When Jesus and his entourage trod the same pilgrim way on that fateful journey, a beggar called Bartimaeus was the one who managed to catch their attention. The account of how he did so, and what immediately follows, is, according to Ched Myers, a decisive paradigm of Christian discipleship.

Bartimaeus was blind. He couldn't see that it was Jesus who was causing the hullabaloo erupting around him, but had to rely for information on those who happened to be next to him in the crowd. Once he knew who it was, he wasted no time beating around the bush; this was his moment, and he seized it. In his naked need he yelled out to Jesus at the top of his voice, his inability to see or to know in exactly which direction to shout, making him shout all the louder. Not only was it at full throttle, but there was a desperate edge to his cry that arrested Jesus' attention amid the clamor all around him.

Significantly, Bartimaeus cries out to Jesus as "Son of David," for this is what they were saying on the streets. In the popular mind, religious and nationalistic hopes were jumbled up together in a mounting expectation that Jesus would sort out everything, including the Romans. He was a chip off the old block, a true "son" of David. We shouldn't look for theological sophistication here. Bartimaeus just felt in his bones that, after untold disappointments and setbacks, Jesus was the new pitcher who would lift the team back to the top and win the World Series; here indeed was the "son of Babe Ruth."

Significantly also, Bartimaeus throws himself on the mercy of Jesus, without question, without condition. It is among the outcasts, those who "know their need of God," that Jesus is acclaimed. These who live on the wrong side of the tracks and wear their hearts on their sleeves, have fewer inhibitions than those with college degrees and a secure job. The latter ask a lot of intelligent questions and end up walking away. They have a yard to tend and an RV to clean out.

Amid the commotion Bartimaeus' voice rings out clear as a bell. "Jesus stood still." Bartimaeus hears Jesus' command "call him," and knows immediately that all will be well. The bystanders show what creeps they are with their words of encouragement to Bartimaeus, moments after having ordered this wailing nobody to hold his tongue. Bartimaeus has no need of their prompting. He comes running.

The rest is history as they say. Bartimaeus experiences restored sight as soon as he hears Jesus' words of acceptance, approval, and blessing. He is at peace with God; he can now become all that God always meant him to be. Not only is his physical sight restored; he sees for the first time what life is about and what he must do to grow into full humanity. He must follow this man; nothing else matters anymore.

The Bartimaeus episode, taking up just seven verses at the end of chapter 10 at the very end of Jesus' journey to Jerusalem, encapsulates the whole process of discipleship. Discipleship begins in blindness and dependence on others, in an encounter with the living Lord that occurs amid noise and clamor and the fickleness of the crowd. Once the moment of stillness has come, when there is just God and you, then we know all will be well, and our response is eager and unconditional.

When Jesus tells Bartimaeus "go," he does not go off on his own, but makes the journey of Jesus his own journey "and followed him on the way." In the end there is no one else worth knowing, nothing else worth doing. When in the fourth Gospel the disciples are given the chance to call it quits and slink off home, Peter says it for Bartimaeus and for all of us: "Lord, to whom can we go? You have the words of eternal life" (John 6:68).

QUESTION:
When my name is called, do I spring up to meet Jesus, or do I ask him a question, playing for time?

PRAYER:
O God, teach us by your Spirit to wait patiently, to speak up powerfully, and to allow nothing to stand in our way when you call us to discipleship through Jesus your Son.

Day 29 ▶

MARK 11:1–11

> *Then they brought the colt to Jesus and threw their cloaks on it; and he sat on it.*

The campaign now quickens its pace as Jesus nears Jerusalem and his showdown with the religious and secular powers. "Jesus comes to Jerusalem not as a pilgrim, in order to demonstrate his allegiance to its temple, but as a popular king ready to mount a non-violent siege on the ruling classes." So says Ched Myers, and basically he is right, although Jesus had no narrow political agenda. He cared nothing for class nor status nor wealth; he cared only for God. His approach to Jerusalem was certainly not that of a humble pilgrim come to be absorbed in the crowd of worshippers content to be carried along on a conveyor belt of ritualized religious observance. Nor was he here for the beer.

Jesus approached Jerusalem in a spirit of confrontation, not against any particular person or group, but against anyone and everyone who failed to honor God. He was outraged by those who evaded God's demands and who cheated their way through their religious life, preening themselves on their observance of the letter while trampling on the spirit. It was not that Jesus set out to make enemies of the ruling classes, whether Sadducee (mainly the priests and lay aristocracy of Jerusalem) or Pharisee (local religious leaders with whom he was more regularly in contact), but that he came to see them as the physical embodiment, through the sacred system they represented, of the tendency in all humankind to replace faith with religion.

In advocating a direct and dynamic relationship with God as "Dad," abrogating the need for religious assault courses and sacerdotal sergeant majors, Jesus was on a collision course with the ecclesiastical establishment. Given their time-hallowed agenda, the religious authorities had no alternative but to condemn him. He was inevitably their enemy because he rendered them obsolete.

Moreover, they were running scared. This self-appointed holy man from the Galilean outback was taking the whole country by storm. He had the whole population eating out of his hand, and now he was at the very gates of the capital. Who could tell what he would do next? What stunts he would pull? What demonstrations and protest marches he would set in motion?

Jesus begins low key. In the self-mocking way he makes arrangements to enter Jerusalem in a parody of a triumphal entry, he runs the risk of being mistaken for an Englishman. Choosing to find a young donkey to ride on, Jesus satirizes all the military liberators of history. The Teacher who has held the country spellbound, who has the city crowds throwing their coats beneath his feet and rampaging through their neighbor's gardens cutting down branches to carpet his processional way, can come up with nothing better than "a colt, the foal of a donkey" (Zechariah 9:9) on which to enter into his triumph.

The ecstatic joy of the crowd who couldn't do enough to show their appreciation was painfully bittersweet to Jesus, who could see only too well what was coming, and how fickle the cheering crowds would prove themselves to be within a matter of days. Here was the lull before the storm, an unreal contrast to the denouement, which was to follow in the same city within the same week. The summer of 1914 was, weather-wise, a particularly glorious one in "England's green and pleasant land"; no one could have guessed the catastrophe that was about to engulf the world.

For Jesus, the day he entered Jerusalem was a gem of a day. Spring flowers covered the hills around the city, and Jerusalem sparkled in the sun. Everyone seemed to be in holiday mood, the town seemingly full of Jewish stand-up comics from Brooklyn, and the laughter was infectious. "Jesus, we *welcome* you!" read the banners; surely everything would turn out right after all?

Tension was mounting, however, and just to make sure we pick up the sense of high drama, Mark finishes the day on a magnificently menacing note. As evening falls, Jesus is last seen going into the temple where he "looked around at everything" and then went out. He cases the joint, and he will be back! Those religious leaders, talking late into the night at the archbishop's palace, have good cause to be worried.

QUESTION:
Do I want to live a life of faith, or am I happier making do with religion?

PRAYER:
O God, as Jesus liberated your people from darkness and despair, may your Holy Spirit now set us free from all that holds us back from surrendering to your love.

Day 30 ▶

MARK 11:12–25

And when the chief priests and the scribes heard it, they kept looking for a way to kill him; for they were afraid of him, because the whole crowd was spellbound by his teaching.

When you are a country boy with business to do in the Big Apple, it's always useful if you can stay with friends on the edge of the city and travel in by subway. It avoids all that nightmare of parking the car. For Jesus, the family home of his old friend Lazarus made a perfect base for him at Bethany, just a few stops beyond Jamaica on the Long Island Railroad.

Next morning Jesus was up early, well before breakfast, and so arrived downtown "hungry." This is the only time throughout his Gospel that Mark mentions Jesus' physical needs, and it may be that he does so as a means of helping to explain the extraordinary scene that follows.

Emerging from the subway onto Wall Street, Jesus wanders along the waterfront at Battery Park where, spotting a healthy looking fig tree leaning over some railings, he thinks he will help himself to some fruit. Finding none on the tree, he is enraged, and curses the tree. The following morning, the disciples see that the tree has shriveled to the ground, never to bear fruit for anyone, ever again. Under the strain of all that was engulfing him, had Jesus just flipped?

The clue to this strange magical incident lies in those sensational stunts pulled by the Old Testament prophets. Those full-blooded characters were often found happily dismembering a yoke of oxen or tearing their best cloak into twelve pieces in order to provide powerful graphics for the catechumenate before the days of PowerPoint presentations.

The timing is important when we recall that the fig tree was an emblem of everything that was wonderful and fruitful about faithful Israel, and its withering a sign of God's judgment. The fig tree incident is thus part and parcel of the event in which Jesus throws down the gauntlet to the religious authorities of Jerusalem. What happens to the fig tree will happen also to the Temple, and less than forty years later, so it does. In AD 70 the Temple was withered to the ground, its hallowed precincts and sacred rituals never to "bear fruit" again for the people of God.

The cleansing of the Temple is deeply symbolic, and its precincts are cleared of more than traders and tables. Jesus does not abandon the Temple—he is to use it as a center for teaching in the days that follow—but he sees it as an institution surviving under occupation. The priestly elite act as if they have God in a box and his people tied up in a straightjacket of mechanical ritual responses, while the traders and money lenders

ensure that the real sacrificial victims are the pilgrims themselves, ripped off to the last cent.

The Temple provided Jesus, at the culmination of his life's
work, with a classic crucial issue on which to make his final challenge to the religious authorities. Here at the very heart of the
Jewish religion was an institution that obscured the God it was
meant to reveal, and that acted as the final blockage to a living
relationship between a thankful people and a loving God.

Throughout his campaigns Jesus had argued it out with local
groups of professionals representing the various vested interests
of the religious establishment; now he must take on the elite at
the center. All along he had striven, not to abrogate the religion
of his people, but to bring it to life as never before. At the heart
of his "new deal" lay the revolution of love and the reversal of
all social norms and ecclesiastical hierarchies in the new community of God where the forgiven and the healed are the first in
the Kingdom. Jesus now strides into the headquarters of those
opposed at every turn to all that he had struggled to establish
and rips their battle plan from the wall. Until the moment he
screamed at the first trader to get the hell out of his Father's
house, he could have slipped away into the country again, pre-
tending he had never meant to have a showdown. Now there is
no turning back; the chips are well and truly down. Reordering
the Temple is the final heresy. This man will have to go.

QUESTION:
What is the final obstacle in my life to God's liberating power
of love?

PRAYER:
O God, in the power of your Spirit, let me not be afraid to go
with Jesus to the heart of the matter and grapple with all that
needs changing, in your Church and in me.

Day 31 ▸

MARK 11:27—12:12

When they realized that he had told this parable against them,
they wanted to arrest him, but they feared the crowd.

The next day Jesus was back again, "walking in the temple" as though nothing had happened. Perhaps he had gotten away with it! The traders seemed to have made a tactical retreat, but they and their protectors in the High Priest's secretariat were furious, and could be seen conferring in small groups in the courtyards, groups that quickly dispersed whenever Jesus drew near.

The authorities kept their cool, knowing they must not fall into the trap of a premature confrontation with Jesus while the crowds were behind him. They needed more evidence to secure a conviction, and their best hope was to engage him in a theological exchange and hope that he would make a slip of the tongue, which could be used against him. Their previous track record gave them no room for optimism, but evidently the "triumph of hope over experience" is not confined to second marriages.

So they get together and decide to field no less than three teams of top players to tackle Jesus on three different areas where he might well be vulnerable and say something, which then could be taken down and used in evidence against him. This was an extremely risky venture. Asking questions of Jesus could be dangerous—you often came away with a flea in your ear, or reeling from a machine-gun burst of Scripture that didn't exactly look good on your résumé.

Jesus (according to Luke at least) had been winning medals for this kind of thing from the age of twelve, and the big boys should have known better than to try that trick. And this was not a good moment. Jesus, no doubt buoyed up by his triumph the previous day, is in even finer form than usual on this bright April morning, and as usual they are hopelessly outwitted.

The first team to enter the arena is a group handpicked from among the "chief priests, the scribes, and the elders," who have been deputized to pin him down on the question of authority. They seek him out as he strolls in the temple court and ask him point blank, "By what authority are you doing these things?" This is a perfectly reasonable question as trick questions go, but they have it turned against them. Having asked it, they should have quit when they were winning, to rightfully claim later that Jesus refused to answer. Instead they get embroiled in a dispute in which they are bound to be outsmarted.

Jesus offers a deal; he will answer their question if they will answer one from him on the same subject of authority, this time about the baptism of John. They have no need to answer it, but they attempt to do so, and get themselves bogged down in a no-win situation, forced in the end to say limply, "We do not know." Here were the temple elite sent away with their tails between their legs, made to look like fools in front of a holiday crowd enjoying the free entertainment, grinning inanely into the TV cameras and waving to Mom back home in Capernaum.

Before they have a chance to disappear, Jesus delivers a *coup de grace* in the form of a story. Jesus takes the picture, familiar from the prophet Isaiah (5:1), of God's community as a vineyard. In his story the owner leases the vineyard to a problem family with severe behavioral difficulties. One after the other, each emissary sent to collect the rent comes to a sticky end, until the owner's beloved son is sent—and is murdered by the tenants. Jesus ends by quoting from Psalm 118 to show that the rejected one will become the key to the future.

The application of this story to God's people Israel, who reject not only the prophets sent to them but even God's beloved

Son, is clear for all to see. The religious authorities recognize only too well that "he had told this parable against them," and they feel humiliated and angry. They consider taking him by force there and then but realize it would be too dangerous to attempt such a thing surrounded by a crowd whom Jesus has eating out of his hand.

So they slink off to lick their wounds, and to talk long into the night as to how perhaps the others may fare better in producing the evidence with which they can crush their troublemaker under the full weight of the law.

QUESTIONS:
In the "vineyard" of my own life, how many messengers of God have I dispatched? Have I rejected even God's own Son?

PRAYER:
O God, when you call me to give account of all that you have entrusted to me, may I never reject your Son, Jesus, who laid down his life for me.

Day 32 ▶

MARK 12:13–17

". . . and to God the things that are God's."

The second team to come running out of the players' tunnel is a combination of "Pharisees and some Herodians," feeling just a little self-conscious in the jazzy new cerise and purple uniforms of their sponsors, the "Bethlehem Brewers." This time there is no pretense about engaging in open and honest debate; the sole purpose of this bunch is to "trap him in what he said," says Mark, this time on the subject of secular authority.

This is a clever move. No matter that the dimwit clergy had made a hash of pinning Jesus down on the religious question, it would be better by far to get Jesus arraigned before the secular power. If only they could glean sufficient evidence from the speeches of Jesus to point the finger at him as some kind of sub- versive *agent provocateur* threatening the stability of the province, perhaps the Roman officials would do their dirty work for them.

Their opening gambit is a rather pathetic attempt to lull Jesus into a false sense of security by flattering him: "Teacher, we know that you are sincere, and show deference to no one." Nothing is more certain to put Jesus on his guard, and he is ready for the trick questions about the divided loyalties that every devout Jew felt when required to pay taxes to the Roman authorities occupy- ing their homeland. The questioners come straight to the point: "Is it lawful to pay taxes to the emperor, or not?" Surely they had him cornered on this one. Whichever way he jumped—into revo- lution or collaboration—they were going to get him.

In reply, Jesus again uses the technique of throwing the question back to his questioners, this time with the help of a visual aid. After chiding them for attempting to test him, he demands of them a coin, gets them to tell him whose head it bears, and concludes with one of his most famous one-liners: "Give to the emperor the things that are the emperor's, and to God the things that are God's." It was an answer that left his hearers "amazed at him," for yet again he had eluded their grasp. They were left stunned.

As things have turned out, it wasn't actually a very good idea for Jesus to answer as he did. Not because of his oppo- nents, but because those who claim to be his followers have abused this text unmercifully ever since.

It has come in very handy indeed for archbishops blessing armies on their way to a little murder, rape, and pillage; for ecclesiastical bureaucrats negotiating a quiet life for the Church in exchange for looking the other way now and again; and for decent educated people turning over in bed when they hear the trucks of the secret police coming for their neighbors in the middle of the night.

It remains a question why, when her hour of triumph came, the Church did not repudiate the state as—to use Augustine's phrase—no more than injustice created into system, and why she reacted so much more strongly against its sexuality than against its violence.

Is this a political commentator analyzing the religious right in today's United States, selling its soul for a seat at the table with the president? No, it's Church historian James Bulloch describing the Church of the early fourth century, mesmerized by the trappings of power into a betrayal of the insights of Jesus. But it's the same story. History shows us the consistent, cunning deviousness of the human mind as (amid loud protestations of Christian allegiance) it successfully evades the basic tenets of Jesus' teaching. Not even Jesus could foresee such apostasy in all its convolutions.

At this moment in the gathering storm in Jerusalem, Jesus' reply was the perfect riposte, because when the secret police played back the tape, they would have heard only commendable loyalty to the mighty emperor on the part of this alleged conspirator.

Those who had been with him for the last three years, who had heard him proclaim obedience to his Father as the one loyalty that overrode all other loyalties—religious or secular— knew what he really meant. Granted that to Jesus, God was all in all and ruled his every thought and action; "the things that are God's" add up to just about everything. The emperor isn't left with very much at all, except perhaps garbage collection.

His questioners realized this too of course, and were furious that the transcript of their exchange would leave Jesus squeaky clean as far as the Roman colonial authorities were concerned.

Nil desperandum. They had as yet one trump card up their sleeve.

QUESTIONS:

When have I "given to the emperor" what really belongs to God? When have I looked the other way in the face of injustice or discrimination?

PRAYER:

O God, by your Spirit, may my loyalty to you be more important to me than anything in the world, even my freedom, through Jesus who gave up his freedom for me.

Day 33 ▶

MARK 12:18–27

> *"For when they rise from the dead, they neither marry nor are given in marriage, but are like angels in heaven."*

The third team to spring into action against Jesus is the most formidable of all: the dreaded Sadducees. Where others have failed, surely they will succeed.

The Sadducees represented the priestly aristocracy of Jerusalem, a cut above those who had already been sent along to argue with Jesus. They were from the top drawer—and knew it. It really was rather unfortunate that they had to lower themselves by entering into a verbal wrangle with this country boy. The others really ought to have sorted it out by now; how trying it is to be surrounded by incompetence! The Sadducees choose theology as their battlefield; not surprising given their particular emphasis on the resurrection, or rather the lack of it. They dream up a trick question about the problem of the woman who had married seven brothers in turn. What on earth would happen at the resurrection; whose wife would she be? Two millennia later we can still hear the sneer in their voices.

The retort of Jesus is surprisingly and unusually hostile: "You know neither the scriptures nor the power of God."

In the Gospels you may come across a "good" Pharisee now and again, but never a "good" priest, and this tendency may go back to Jesus himself. It is not difficult to see why Jesus the Galilean peasant layman, claiming a charismatic religious authority impossible to categorize, and the high priestly families of Jerusalem, whose power base depended on everyone sticking to the ritual rules, were doomed to unrelieved hostility.

Jesus points the Sadducees to a new world beyond death where the categories and relationships of this passing world will be swallowed up in the life of God. He is talking to a small group of Sadducees, but speaking to us.

I remember exactly at which traffic light it was where my passenger, a lovely lady from our faith community, not long widowed, turned to me with the desperate question, "I will see my George again, won't I?"

"When they rise from the dead, they neither marry nor are given in marriage." This is Jesus' answer, and we don't really believe him. We would rather hang on to the folk religion that reassures us heaven will be one long reunion. Life will go on just as before, with all the same categories and departments, only this time our batteries won't run flat. In its ministry to the bereaved, the Church has long colluded with this false expectation, and I have played my part by releasing into the atmosphere all those little prayer cards with texts about the departed having popped into the next room to wait for their loved ones to catch up with them.

The domestic arrangements of heaven are a topic that non-Christians find endlessly fascinating (second only to finding out how clergy move parishes, but that's for another time), but Christians should know better. Jesus made it quite clear that the entry point to the Kingdom of God is not at some hazy checkpoint in the blue beyond, but here and now, in the details of daily life. Once we have entered into a life of union with God through Jesus in the Spirit, then heaven has already begun. We should therefore be too busy enjoying this party to worry about the arrangements for the next.

So how did we get ourselves into this mess? We end up being either unspeakably callous or peddling palliatives that will help no one to grow up into God. Our good news is surely that heaven is *better* than anything we have ever known or dreamt of here, that God's promises exceed all that we can desire.

My own guess is that it will be something like going to the Super Bowl; we are one of a vast crowd without which the event would be meaningless, but when our team scores the winning touchdown in the final seconds, we are caught up in something bigger than ourselves; we are lost in the ecstatic moment, oblivious to those around us, yet aware of them. Heaven isn't run by Carthusian monks, with a host of individuals in separate cells gazing at God; it's more likely that the football fans are in charge, for we are to be caught up *together* in one big celebration, oblivious to one another in the ecstatic moment of the presence of God.

QUESTIONS:

What is really important in my dream of heaven? Is it having forever who and what I have now, or is it experiencing the presence of God?

PRAYER:

O God, when your Spirit kindles our hearts to love, remind us that you invented love, and created those we love, and that we have nothing to fear, now or beyond death, because of Jesus.

Day 34 ▶

MARK 12:28-37

"You are not far from the kingdom of God."

Having warded off three sets of antagonists, Jesus is approached yet again, but this time it is by a lone scribe with a genuine question. Jesus emerges from an exhausting session with the tenth-grade remedial group—out to make trouble and with no intention of learning anything—and crosses the corridor to enter the different world of high school seniors intent on entrance to the Ivy League, where there is real encounter, comradeship, and an eagerness to learn.

The scribe comes to Jesus because, having observed the three previous encounters with the authorities, he saw "that he answered them well." He is impressed, and wants to take things further from a position of honest inquiry. So those antagonistic exchanges weren't a waste of time after all; the questioners up front may have been asking questions to which they already knew the answers, but in the background, quietly watching and waiting, was the potential disciple whose quest for the truth made it all worthwhile. With God, one out of a hundred is "success rate" enough.

At first hearing, this scribe seems like a bit of a creep who inexplicably achieves good marks for simply repeating parrot-fashion what Jesus tells him. It is the small print, however, that holds the key. Having virtually repeated, word for word, what Jesus has just said, the scribe then adds ten little words, affirming that to love God and one's neighbor is "much more important than all whole burnt offerings and sacrifices."

The scribe has taken in the teaching of Jesus and applied it to his own situation and religious culture. He has immediately worked out the practical consequences of his newfound insight into the mystery of God; there is no danger of it staying locked up in his head as pure theory. "You are not far from the kingdom of God"; thus Jesus warmly commends him for his discernment, and his working out for himself that, once we grasp hold of the love and forgiveness of God, then the whole cultic system is superfluous.

Coming so soon after his disputation with the champions of that cultic system, those with a vested interest in perpetuating what Ched Myers calls "the redemptive/symbolic system of debt represented in the temple," the encounter with this humble scribe must have delighted Jesus' heart. In addition to replacing perpetual indebtedness with forgiveness, Jesus had another major item on the agenda of reform. He was anxious to reinterpret the whole idea of the Messiah as a Davidic king.

The rather convoluted verses referring to the relationship

between the Christ and King David appear to us now as a little bit of internal Jewish stuff that we can easily skip. They give us the key, however, to how Jesus understood his own vocation as the Anointed One of God.

The old imperial vision—conceived in disobedience to God in demanding a king in the first place (1 Samuel 10:19)—continues to seduce Israel with its mirage of earthly power and conquest. Talk of "sovereignty" always goes down well with the voters but is symptomatic of a nation with a past and no present.

In Jesus' own generation there was no future to be had in the continued beating of the old militaristic drum, harking back to the good old days of David when Israel threw its weight about. Indeed the posturing of the freedom fighters would lead to the total humiliation of Israel and the destruction of the Temple within a few decades of Jesus' lifetime.

The manner of his entry into Jerusalem, parodying the triumphant liberator, had made his position clear; and he now sets out to wean his compatriots away from raw jingoism into a new understanding of the Messiah's role, in which God alone is sovereign.

"David himself calls him Lord; so how can he be his son?" Thus Jesus demands that the Davidic tradition be subsumed under a theocracy in which the Anointed One is understood as servant rather than soldier.

QUESTIONS:
Do God's commandments stay in my head or move to my heart? Am I any good at "applied" as well as "pure" Christianity?

PRAYER:
O God, by the teaching of your Son and in the power of your Spirit, help me to enthrone you alone as sovereign Lord over everything I am and everything I have.

Day 35 ▶

MARK 12:38–44

"Beware of the scribes, who like to walk around in long robes, and to be greeted with respect in the marketplaces, and to have the best seats in the synagogues and places of honor at banquets!"

Two bits of teaching immediately follow, which spell out the salient characteristics of this Kingdom of God revealed by Jesus—humility and generosity—precisely those that the Church has always had the greatest difficulty in embracing. "The greatest challenge to us religious people," wrote Sheila Cassidy, "is not how to spread the Gospel but how to live it."

Humility is the starting point because it is the basic building block in living the new life, one that helps us look at the immensity of creation with reverence and awe and wonder, with an awareness of our smallness.

"Drink me" said the label on the bottle that Alice found at the bottom of the well, and once she had drunk, she became small enough to get through the tiny hole into the beautiful garden, into her Wonderland. We must drink deep of "the cup that I drink" if we are to become as little children, small enough to enter the Kingdom.

Seigfried Sassoon declared that "if a man has loved so much as a grapefruit, God will save him." If we can begin the day by delighting in God's gifts at the breakfast table, perhaps there's a chance we may live for a few hours at least not consumed by self-interest. Humility lies in our waking up each morning believing, not that the world is very lucky to have us around, but that we are very blessed to be here.

In that television interview just before he died, the playwright Dennis Potter described his humility (although he didn't use the word, humility it was) before the plum blossom bursting out beneath his window at Ross on Wye:

> Instead of saying, "Oh, that's a nice blossom" looking out through the window when I'm writing, it is the whitest, frothiest, blossomiest blossom that there could ever be.

The most wondrous thing in all creation is a fellow human being, and Jesus gave us enough clues in his teaching for us to know how carefully and humbly we must proceed here. It is "the least"—the unlikeliest, the least attractive, the smelliest, the most disfigured, the most embarrassing—who are our most regular and real encounter with the Son of Man. Why is it that I always remember that bit from Hebrews about "entertaining angels unawares" *after* I've shown my annoyance at having my hurried lunch at my desk interrupted for the third time?

The most difficult aspect of all is to be humble before ourselves. Any diocesan job that involves visiting lots of parishes soon brings one face-to-face with the crippling self-importance of so many of the clergy (and their ambitious spouses!). Perhaps before too long a research scientist somewhere will patent the "Acme Clerical Pomposometer," which will let off an almighty racket every time a member of the clerical profession reminds one of their doctorate, canonry, or pride of place on the presiding bishop's Christmas card list.

At least those future clergy emerging from Cuddesdon (a seminary near Oxford) during the 1960s received a basic training in not taking oneself too seriously. For us, the Munn's Memorial Gallery was of immense significance in priestly formation. Situated in a tiny third floor restroom, it boasted an incredible array of objects to which were attached business cards from the princes of the Church. Thus it was that a bedpan "with the compliments of the Bishop of Oxford" or a pair of corsets "donated" by the Dean of Windsor would help us keep everything in perspective. Humor is the spouse of humility, for it keeps breaking through whenever we begin to take ourselves too seriously—before others do the breaking through for us.

Jesus knew full well that generosity, not cleanliness, is next to godliness, because generosity is the essence of the nature of God. That is why the poor widow is the heroine of the Kingdom in this section of Mark's story. "I observed that Jones is that rarity, a man who pours wine for others when his own glass is full" is a good description of generosity from the cooking section of a Sunday newspaper. The poor widow would have done just the same had she had any wine to pour; it's all a question of basic disposition of the soul.

There is an absolutely invariable correlation between vinegar in the veins and moths in the wallet. As D. L. Moody put it, "The last part of a man to be converted is his pocket." Conversely, those whose generosity (if known) would blow one's mind, will be the same quiet, humble, and willing people always ready to say yes, always ready with a smile, whose qualities make a congregation a community. I'd even rig an annual meeting to get that "poor widow" on my vestry!

QUESTION:

Is there anything in my life at the moment that is causing me to take myself too seriously, to be a little too aware of my dignity, to imagine that it all depends on me?

PRAYER:

O God, by your Spirit keep me humble, that I may delight in your creation, serve those you have given me to love, and smile at myself in my frailty, for Jesus' sake.

Day 36 ▶

MARK, CHAPTER 13

"Not one stone will be left here upon another;
all will be thrown down."

This was one of those days when no one could get near him. Jesus was feeling very down, and no one could lift his spirits or shake him out of it. He knew the bubble must burst very soon, and when he lay awake at night, he couldn't help wondering whether it had all been worthwhile.

Bless their hearts, the disciples do their best, trying to snap him out of it by donning their Bermuda shorts, Hawaiian shirts, and shades; strapping on their cameras (Judas has somehow acquired a camcorder; don't ask how); and trying to get Jesus excited about the big city sights with an "Ooh, just look at that!" session. "Boss! Just look at those wonderful stones and wonderful buildings!"

Jesus just is not in the mood. He's seen his tenth Byzantine church that morning, his feet are killing him, and the over-excited jabbering of these hillbilly disciples is beginning to get on his nerves. Right now he could do with an ice-cold beer.

"Buildings? Hrmmph! They won't last a week come the revolution!" It's what you might call a conversation stopper, and the disciples slink away like children who see the present they have so carefully wrapped up on Mother's Day cast into a corner. They go and find a wall to sit on, out of the way, and eat their peanut butter and jelly sandwiches in dejected silence. Not even Matthew's kettle-cooked potato chips could console them.

The boss sits alone on a bench near the coin-operated telescope at the vantage point on the Mount of Olives. Motionless, he stares across to the Temple, symbol of the powerful and all-pervasive vested interests ranged against him and closing in on him. He wonders whether he has what it takes to go through with it. He longs for Nazareth. Four of the disciples—the two sets of brothers: James and John, Simon and Andrew—feel bad about him being on his own, and sidle awkwardly up to Jesus, sitting down alongside him in silence.

Eventually they manage to blurt out something. They tell him that he has them worried now; if everything is going to collapse around them, how long do they have before catastrophe strikes?

Jesus is warmed by their companionship and tries to explain something of his own vocation, into which those who remain close to him will enter. At the heart of it lies the mystery as to why the role of the suffering servant-messiah should arouse such animosity and hatred, cause such bitter division within the same household, attract so many bogus claimants to his throne, and be surrounded by such tumult and violence. "This is but the beginning of the birthpangs." All Jesus can do is warn his closest followers of what must inevitably come, prepare them for the worst, and remind them of the inner resources, not of this world, that they have at their disposal. Above all, they will have the Holy Spirit, who will speak eloquently for them (like Aaron for Moses) when sheer terror makes their mouths go dry.

Keep awake are therefore the final words of this intimate lunchtime instruction session on a park bench on the Mount of Olives. Jesus himself, and those who follow after him, must be constantly on "red alert" against the temptation to cave in, to accept the world's way of sorting things out, to suppose that the end justifies the means and that two wrongs can make a right. "And what I say to you I say to all: Keep awake."

They have an impossible task, but there is nothing to fear provided they continue to live in union with God as Father, empowered by the Spirit that will be released in them by their association with Jesus. Explaining something particularly difficult to someone else serves to clarify our mind and strengthen our resolve. Jesus feels greatly comforted and strengthened by these moments with his closest friends, and there is a spring in his step again as he leads them over to the others before all those kettle-cooked potato chips have disappeared.

QUESTIONS:
Have I fully understood that my discipleship of Jesus will inevitably cause, at some point or other, total mayhem in my life? Am I ready for it?

PRAYER:
O God, may your Son's command to us to keep awake not be wasted on us, so that in your Spirit we may never be taken by surprise by the cost of discipleship.

Day 37 ▸

MARK 14:1–11

> *"Truly I tell you, wherever the good news is proclaimed in the whole world, what she has done will be told in remembrance of her."*

In these last days, Jesus lived on death row. He knew it would not be long before they came for him. The fact that he was theoretically free to arrange his own "stay of execution" by melting away into the countryside only served to twist the knife. He lived only to obey his Father's will, and he could see no other way than that of sacrifice. Words and deeds of love had not proved enough; they wanted blood. Although still a "free" man, Jesus was condemned to death. As Helen Prejean has powerfully described:

> the essential torture of the death penalty is not finally the physical method of death . . . but happens when conscious human beings are condemned to death and die a thousand, thousand times before they die.

Jesus died many deaths that last week in Bethany, and amid this inner turmoil, was glad to accept an act of kindness in the form of a dinner invitation from a leper he knew called Simon. Here in the company of friends, he might at least be able to push to the back of his mind for a moment the dark thoughts of the how and when of death.

The evening was going well. Jesus was beginning to unwind, and Simon was just wondering whether he could get away with telling the one about the rabbi and the exotic dancer when in bursts this woman, bold as brass. This was just not done; no one should be allowed to burst in on a private dinner like this, least of all a woman. The other guests didn't bother to keep their voices down, "Come on, Simon, get rid of her!"

But the woman was not the kind to be gotten rid of easily. She had a bit of a wild look about her, but also a natural authority. The men coughed rather nervously and shifted in their seats. They hoped it wasn't going to take too long; the next course looked delicious.

She never spoke a word, but calmly walked up to where Jesus was sitting and stood over him. Simon edged forward, ready to spring lest she should try to harm his guest in any way—you could never be too careful.

Simon need not have worried. From the folds of her cloak she produced, not a hand grenade, but a jar of perfumed oil—the very best that money could buy—and she proceeded to anoint Jesus. Not timidly, but with a grand gesture worthy of the prophets, she smashed the alabaster container on the tiled floor, and filling her cupped hands with oil, poured it over his head. Jesus recognizes immediately the poignancy of the moment, and declares it to be an anointing for his own burial. It is also an anointing fit for a king, and Jesus appreciated the irony of this "royal" anointing so thoroughly in keeping with his "royal" procession into Jerusalem. In the same vein of parody, here is an anointing not by a great prophet on a mountainside before the massed armies of Israel, but by an unknown woman in someone's dining room before a few friends. It fits the bill perfectly, and Jesus is warm and generous in his thanks, shaming the others.

This ridiculous playacting and waste of precious resources is the final straw for Judas. He wants to see matters brought to a head once and for all, and now sets the wheels in motion to force a showdown. It is at this point that the film music changes mood and tempo, and that shots of the drunken driver getting into his car are juxtaposed with those of a four-year-old playing in the street; you know something absolutely awful is about to happen, and you can't bear to look.

QUESTION:
What bold and extravagant act have I done this week that could be described as "something beautiful for God"?

PRAYER:

O God, give us the courage to obey your will, that by your Spirit
we may do the outrageous deed of love by which the Good News
of Jesus is preached to the whole world.

Day 38 ▸

MARK 14:12–25

*"Where do you want us to go and make the preparations
for you to eat the Passover?"*

That's the funny thing about Passover; one minute it's months
away, and the next minute it's tomorrow and nothing's been
done! And this one was going to be special.

With one foot in heaven, Jesus tends to leave the practical
details—like getting the truck registered and insured—to the
guys, and they want the Passover arrangements fixed. For once,
Jesus has it all worked out, down to the last detail, with a lot
of Robert B. Parker-type instructions about a rendezvous at
South Street Station with a mystery man wearing a white car-
nation who will conduct them to a safe house on the Back Bay.
It all seems a bit over the top to them, but they dutifully go
along with it and, fair enough, they "found everything as he had
told them; and they prepared the Passover meal." The venue
turned out to be a spacious upstairs sitting room in a lovely
house overlooking the Charles River (the boss's contacts—high
or low—never ceased to amaze them), and they set to with a will
to make everything as perfect as possible.

For once they all pulled together as a real team, and it reminded the Zebedee brothers of the time, years ago, when they had gone youth hosteling in the Golan Heights, peeling spuds for fifty guests every night. Matthew, James, and John (accompanied by Judas, who always wore the money belt) went down to Trader Joe's to buy in everything they could think of, and while Peter and Andrew clattered about the kitchen, the others laid the table and arranged the furniture. Thaddeus (always a bit of a hopeless case, best kept out of the way of anything breakable) was asked to go and find some flowers for the table—and not to hurry back.

It was nearly evening by the time everything was shipshape, and they set off in high spirits to meet Jesus at the subway station and bring him back in triumph to this little nest they had created with such pleasure. They ushered him upstairs and waited with baited breath for his approval and affirmation, as excited as a kindergarten class desperately holding up their crayon masterpieces for the attention of their adored teacher.

They couldn't help feeling rather pleased with themselves. Everything looked splendid, and even Thaddeus's tulips (the flower seller must have seen him coming) had been propped up to look half-alive. Jesus led the customary prayers of blessing, and the meal began.

It was a lovely occasion; the food they had taken so much trouble with exceeded all expectations, and they felt for one another a deep bond of affection as they recalled all they had been through together since last Passover. This was indeed a feast to remember.

Suddenly Jesus goes and spoils it all! First he turns on the assembled company and accuses one of them of being a traitor who would literally "kiss and tell" with disastrous consequences. Everything went deadly quiet; you could have cut the

atmosphere with a knife. Then a jabber of incredulous protestations of innocence followed by suspicious glances round the
table, nudged elbows, and muttered accusations. The whole
meal is ruined. They begin to push their plates away.

After a while Jesus continues eating, and they attempt to
follow suit. Then he goes and does it again! Just as a kind of
normality was returning, Jesus carries out before their very eyes
a macabre prophetic act with the bread and the cup, announcing his own imminent death. With Mark there is no bothering
with commands about doing this again; this is a prophetic act
of the present moment to spell out to the disciples with simple
and utterly terrifying clarity what is going to happen to Jesus
before many hours have passed.

Perhaps we need a little more of Mark and a little less of
John when it comes to making the Eucharist real. Or, as an old
school pal of mine used to say, "less talk, more do." Less docile
adoration, more heart-stopping encounter. Getting caught in
an upper room with Jesus makes skydiving or white-water raft-
ing look like a Sunday school picnic. He shows us in this critical prophetic act that we go out from his presence to be broken
and bled. We mustn't mind when he spoils this nice private
meal we are having with our friends!

QUESTION:
Am I so busy helping to get the room ready that I don't see
Jesus come in, or hear what he says across the table?

PRAYER:
O God, teach me not to mind when Jesus interrupts with his
talk of sacrifice the nice meal we are having with our friends. By
your Spirit may we follow him outside into the waiting world.

Day 39 ▸

MARK 14:26-42

*He took with him Peter and James and John, and began
to be distressed and agitated.*

There is no more eating after that. Most of them realize what
is going on and what must be done, even if they have no heart
for it. Jesus closes with a prayer and a hymn, and leads them
out to the park overlooking the city. They sit down in a group
around him for the last "plenary session" they will ever have
together.

Despite his conviction that God his Father will somehow
vindicate him, and that he will return to Galilee, Jesus is dis-
consolate, weighed down at the thought of being abandoned
by every single one of these men. The glib protestations of
do-or-die loyalty led by (guess who?) hotheaded but well-
meaning Peter only serve to intensify the pain. He then led
them further into the city, aware that they must be nearer the
center of action if the final scenes of the drama are to be en-
acted. Boston Common would never do; it had to be Fenway
Park. Here he took aside the inner core—Peter, James, and John—
and made no secret of his distress. They are asked to keep watch
while he goes off to be alone.

Gethsemane was the pits. Here was the true Passion before
ever a hand was raised against him. It was here and now that the
final decision had to be made whether to die, to run, or to light
the fuse of revolt. The true agony is one of indecision. Once the
way ahead is clearly determined, however unthinkable it may

be, we somehow summon the courage to go through with it. It's the not knowing that tears him apart.

We have been taught from Sunday school onward to think of Jesus as He-who-was-in-control. In Gethsemane Jesus was portrayed kneeling in earnest and reverent prayer, his gaze steady, his garments as immaculate as ever.

But in Gethsemane he lost control. "He threw himself on the ground" Mark says, and became "distressed and agitated." When we use those words, especially of a man, it's a polite way of saying that he was sobbing uncontrollably, pounding the ground with his fists, ranting at the skies. His robes got filthy.

As with most of us, however, anger, once vented, gives way to calm. Using the most intimate form of address to God as his own dear Father, Jesus prays that if possible he might be spared arrest and execution. But he desires an answer only on God's terms.

Thus even in the depths of his despair, Jesus does not cease to teach us. Here is the nature of prayer laid out for us. Gethsemane puts to rest once and for all those extraordinary assertions that Christians have only to pray in Jesus' name for all things to be granted them. This is plainly nonsense—we don't seem to have emptied many hospitals by this method yet, and it is dangerous, guaranteed to raise false expectations leading directly to nervous breakdowns among the gullible.

Of course God answers prayer, but not to order. Insofar as we submit to the sovereignty of the Father and enter with Jesus into union with him by laying down our own lives in the power of the Spirit, then we too will experience the release of the healing, reconciling love of God. Amazing things will begin to happen amid even the most cataclysmic circumstances. They will happen even at Golgotha.

Gethsemane takes us to the heart of the mystery of intercessory prayer at the same time it takes us to the heart of Jesus. Even he who lived constantly in union with the will of the Father prays a prayer to which the immediate answer must be "no."

But the "no" is sufficient answer; Jesus is now quite sure what must be done. The indecision is over; he can face the rest, knowing it is the Father's will, that there is no other way. He has passed through despair and distress into quiet acceptance: "Get up, let us be going."

QUESTION:
When I feel betrayed, do I cover it up with a seemly reverent prayer, or is my relationship with God real enough for me to shout?

PRAYER:
O God, teach me by your Spirit to submit myself, with Jesus, to the sovereignty of your love, that even when the answer to my prayer is "no," your will may be done on earth.

Day 40 ►

MARK 14:43–51

> *A certain young man was following him.*

Even as he speaks with his newfound confidence, Jesus is rudely interrupted. There is great commotion and noise as a crowd of people suddenly comes crashing through the undergrowth.

They carry flaming torches and are armed to the teeth, and to keep up their spirits in the face of the unknown, they holler and shout, swagger and curse; they are overreaction personified.

Now is the final moment of choice for Jesus. Surrounded by this howling mob, ridiculous in its inappropriateness for the task in hand, he is confronted by Judas, the one that got away, ready with his signal of identification.

One look would have done it, one restraining hand, one sharp cry for help to those who stood nearby awaiting only a signal. But he said and did nothing, and in that split-second decision, sealed the new deal with God.

There was no trouble; it all went quietly. The only casualty was the High Priest's slave, who lost an ear in a scuffle with one of Jesus' followers who had somehow smuggled a sword into the garden. How difficult for us, fallen creatures that we are, not to give three cheers for this full-blooded blow in the cause of right, and not to be rather pleased that Mark has no record of the ear being sewn back on (only Luke the physician seeing fit to provide a happy ending).

But of course we would be wrong. Violence and revenge are not to be the way. Jesus knows that all would be lost the moment he summoned support. His "rescue package" has to be valid for all people for all time, irrespective of circumstance. His good news is not for those with big battalions or loud voice, but for the weak and helpless, all whose lives are considered cheap on the world market. Only love would do.

Jesus cannot resist a comment on the authorities' ridiculous overkill—so typical of the reaction of corrupt and frightened regimes silencing dissidence down the centuries. He has never hidden himself, never raised a finger against any person; why the need for helmeted riot police, tear gas, dogs, and all?

He knows it is a waste of breath, however, and is resigned to his fate: "But let the scriptures be fulfilled."

At this point comes the nadir of Jesus' whole life's work: the men whom he had handpicked, commissioned, trained, loved, and laughed with, "all of them deserted him and fled." After their "vehement" protestations of loyalty, Jesus watches them scurrying away into holes like rabbits scared out of their wits. At this moment Jesus drains the dregs of his cup of bitter suffering.

There is one little sign of hope. Like a wildflower blooming beside the body of a dying soldier, it is of no help to the fallen, but is nevertheless a sign pregnant with new life and hope.

"A young man" wearing "nothing but a linen cloth" follows Jesus. He can be of no use. He is one unarmed youth facing a squad of soldiers; there is nothing he can do, except be there, hiding himself, peeping round corners, shadowing the action. But he is there.

Soon the soldiers spot him and try to seize him, but they succeed only in grabbing him by his garment, and he evades capture by fleeing naked into the night.

It would be nice to think that this was indeed Mark himself, as legend would have it, setting his seal on this eyewitness account. If so, we understand why Mark toiled for years thereafter to bring to birth this most vivid and direct account of the story of Jesus.

No matter—this last tiny incident before Jesus is led away to the kangaroo court, this final stop on the campaign trail, has within it the seed with which God will again enrich the earth and make it fruitful.

The young man is an outsider—not a chosen disciple—who follows to the end when all others have deserted, and who ends up losing everything that he has for a glimpse of Jesus.

Whoever he was, he was not one of the twelve, but he was a true disciple.

QUESTION:

At what point will I give up and flee, and how much will I want to take with me?

PRAYER:

O God, may the Spirit empower me to hold on to Jesus when all others have forsaken him and fled, that in losing my life I might find it in him.

Epilogue

MARK 16:1–8

That was the end of the campaign trail, but it wasn't the end of the story. After the hideous events of Jesus' final hours, subjected to mockery (the cruelest torture of all), flogging, and execution as a common criminal, his body was buried in a tomb made available by an establishment figure with the courage to stand alone in doing an act of kindness. And that was that.

The disciples went into hiding, consumed by self-loathing and paralyzed by fear, but with hope-against-hope breaking through now and again that perhaps somehow something of what Jesus had promised would happen, would happen. There had been all that strange talk of his about rising again . . . but what could it mean?

Significantly it was the weak ones, the outsiders—not the

chosen and trusted disciples—who came to the tomb to do something beautiful for Jesus whom they could not believe was dead.

As they went the women chided one another for not getting one or two of the useless men out of bed to open the tomb for them by rolling away the boulder with which it had been sealed two days before. They needn't have worried. To their astonishment and dismay, they found that the boulder had already been moved. Had someone broken in? Desecrated the tomb? Violated the body? This was the final straw.

Fearless in their indignation, they go into the tomb, stooping beneath the low ceiling, and are greeted by a messenger of God, a "young man."

Ched Myers points out a fascinating pattern here in the Greek words used in the final episodes of Mark's story. In the very last incident before Jesus is taken away for trial, the "young man" *(neaniskos)* flees the garden, abandoning his "linen cloth" *(sindon)*. In the very first incident after Jesus' death and burial, the same two words reappear in the Greek text: A "linen cloth" is bought by Joseph of Arimathea with which to wrap the body of Jesus, and a "young man" greets the women with news of Jesus' new life.

Perhaps things are never quite as neat as that, but why worry? In a powerful way the "young man" and his "linen cloth" enfold the story of Jesus' final hours, popping up like a couple of bookends at either end of the Passion narrative to show us the transforming power of the invincible love of God.

Setting aside the "happy ending" (v. 9 onward) that some well-meaning soul couldn't resist adding later (and from which, very strangely, the Roman Lectionary chooses the Gospel passage for St. Mark's Day), we see how Mark's ending at verse 8 hits just the right note.

Mark eschewed all frills at the beginning of his story, and

he eschews them at the end. The Gospel ends in disarray as the women flee the tomb in "terror and amazement." The Risen Lord is announced, but he is not seen. Jesus is a mystery. Exactly who he was, where he came from, and where he has gone remains obscure. His presence lives on, and his followers will be empowered to enter into his relationship with God and to change the world. That's it, really.

What a pity that later generations of Christians, anxious to provide employment for out-of-work theologians and over-ambitious prelates, allowed "Christology" to appear in the religious education syllabus, losing sleep and shedding blood over the distinction between *homoousion* and *homoiousion*.

All we need to know is that in the person of this man Jesus, the love of God was released into the world as never before or since; that in him the splendor of full and free humanity was revealed as never before or since; that through him the path through death into life is opened up for all who enter into his relationship with God as Father.

Mark now says "over to you"; the next chapters of the good news according to Mark are for us to write. We take it from here. No wonder then that the last word of his Gospel is "afraid." It is indeed a terrifying thing to fall into the hands of the living God, but in encountering Jesus through the eyes of Mark, that's just what we've done.

Group Questions ▶

The following questions are offered as a resource to any group wishing to use this little book as a shared exercise, for example, during Lent.

Five weeks' supply is provided—five "sorties" in the campaign of Jesus—which means you will be squeezing eight days into seven, but then that's what it feels like for most of us most of the time.

First Sortie (Day 1 to Day 8)

1. Look at how Mark introduces Jesus to us, as compared with the writers of the other three Gospels. Does Mark give us all we need to know about Jesus?
2. If we had only Mark's account, what difference would it make to our Christian belief and discipleship?

Second Sortie (Day 9 to Day 16)

1. What are the priorities in Jesus' own campaign, and how clearly are these reflected in the program of our faith community, locally and nationally?
2. At what points have we been surprised or scandalized by Mark's account over the last eight days?

Third Sortie (Day 17 to Day 24)

1. Do we include confrontation and rejection as part and parcel of the Christian life, or are we surprised and resentful when we encounter reversals and setbacks?

2. Looking at the ups and downs of the Twelve recounted by Mark over the last eight days, what can we learn to help us in our task of becoming better disciples, within this group and in our local faith community?

Fourth Sortie (Day 25 to Day 32)

1. Which are the hard sayings of Jesus that we find difficult to accept, and why?
2. What would happen to our faith community if our "temple" was destroyed? What would be the basic building blocks with which we would start again in our common relationship with God?

Fifth Sortie (Day 33 to Day 40)

1. How important are the domestic arrangements of heaven? Is our experience of the glory of God a present reality or a future hope?
2. Who exactly was Jesus, anyway?

Works Cited ►

This list is by no means complete. I have drawn extensively from the commonplace I have kept for many years, wherein many sources are not noted.

Borg, Marcus J. *Meeting Jesus Again for the First Time.* Harper, 1994.

Bulloch, James. *Pilate to Constantine.* St. Andrew, 1981.

Cassidy, Sheila. *The Tablet.* April 1995.

Huck, Gabe. *Liturgy with Style and Grace.* Liturgy Training Publications, 1984.

Meier, John. *A Marginal Jew.* Vol. 1. Doubleday, 1991.

Myers, Ched. *Binding the Strong Man.* Orbis, 1991.

Potter, Dennis. "Without Walls," an interview with Dennis Potter, Channel 4 Television, April 1994.

Prejean, Helen. *The Tablet.* April 1995.